Evidence for the 1864 John Brown Family Camp Corral Sketch

Claims & Findings

Compiled by

Janelle Molony
Nicholas R. Cataldo
Larry Cundall

© 2024, Janelle Molony

 M Press Publishing

Copyright © 2024 by Janelle Molony
Official Author Website: www.JanelleMolony.com
All rights reserved. No part of this book, including images, may be reproduced, or used in any manner, without written permission of the copyright owner except for the use of quotations in a book review or as permitted under fair use laws.

ISBN: 979-8-9905118-0-4
Non-Fiction: U.S. History / Civil War / Reference / Academic / Education / Westward Emigration

Evidence for the 1864 John Brown Family Camp Corral Sketch

Table of Contents

PREFACE 1

EVIDENCE AND ITEMS OF PROVENANCE FROM JANELLE MOLONY 3

    RELATED ATTACHMENTS 7

EVIDENCE AND ITEMS OF PROVENANCE FROM NICHOLAS R. CATALDO 33

    RELATED ATTACHMENTS 34

EVIDENCE AND ITEMS OF PROVENANCE FROM LARRY CUNDALL 43

    RELATED ATTACHMENTS 47

Evidence for the 1864 John Brown Family Camp Corral Sketch

Preface

It is presently believed that a covered wagon train camp corral sketch made in the *1864 Diary of Mrs. Sarah Jane Rousseau* contains the only known illustration of the Brown Train, as led by Salmon Brown (son of Underground Railroad Engineer and Pre-Civil War Abolitionist, John Brown), while on their 1863-1864 journey from North Elba, New York to Red Bluff, California. Extensive research has been compiled on this trip, including the specific movements of the Brown Train (AKA "The New York Train") and select experiences of the family members from the timeframe when this camp sketch was drawn. Interested readers are encouraged to view those conclusions in the nonfiction, *Emigrant Tales of the Platte River Raids* (M Press, 2023).

The original camp sketch within the *1864 Diary of Mrs. Sarah Jane Rousseau* is currently in the Molony family estate and remains inaccessible to the public, outside of photographs taken by Nicholas R. Cataldo (with family permission). The diary is a small, leather-bound book with lightly penciled-in sketches and flowers pressed between the pages. A complete, descendant-authenticated transcription of the diary was published in 2023 *without* the image of the sketch being referenced in this material. Extra care has been taken (and time given) towards studying the original document, collecting evidence, and other necessary efforts to establish provenance for the claims made herein. I believe the release of this information and related images will be a breakthrough in current scholarship and, in my opinion, an exceptional discovery worthy of national recognition.

The images included in this book are either property of the author-contributors, used with permission, or are presented in accordance with Fair Use practices as educational illustrations necessary for academic, historical, and critical review.

Janelle Molony
3rd Great-Granddaughter of Sarah Rousseau, Trail Diarist and Sketch Artist of 1864

Evidence for the 1864 John Brown Family Camp Corral Sketch

Evidence for the 1864 John Brown Family Camp Corral Sketch

Evidence and Items of Provenance from Janelle Molony

*Personal contact information has been reduced or entirely redacted from this public document.

2/8/2024

Provenance Claim Re: July 9-10, 1864 Pella Company Camp Sketch with the family of Pre-Civil War Abolitionist John Brown.

I, Janelle Molony, hereby declare the camp sketch found on the back pages of Sarah Jane Rousseau's 1864 diary **(See Attachment A)** to be an authentic reproduction of a camp corral in Glendo, Wyoming that includes 9 wagons/vehicles belonging to the Pella Company and 3 wagons/vehicles belonging to Salmon Brown (son of pre-Civil War Abolitionist John Brown, veteran of "Bleeding Kansas" and organizer of 1859 Harpers Ferry Siege and other notable events).

Specific evidence for the claim:

I. **It is common knowledge that the Brown Train was traveling west from New York in 1863-1864 with three covered wagons.**
   1. Source evidence for this claim comes from the primary records of Salmon and Abbie Brown:

      - Brown, Abbie C. Hinckley. Letter to Mrs. [John] Brown [Jr.]. October 9, 1864.

        Additional Commentary – A direct quote from this letter to Wealthy C. Hotchkiss (1829-1911) in Put-On-Bay, Ohio from Abbie in Red Bluff, California reads: "We threw up our contract and in April, with our emigrant wagons and with oxen and cows, we made another start for that country. We had <u>three wagons,</u> one for our family, consisting of Mr. Brown and myself and two children, another for Mr. Brown's mother and sisters and one wagon with six Spanish Merino sheep. The last two wagons were driven by two young men who wished to go to California and drove the team for their board." **(See Attachment B)**

      - Brown, Abbie C. Hinckley. "Across the Plains in the Early 60's as Told by one who Participated in the Stirring Events of That Adventureous Western Era." Lake Placid News, September 29, 1916, 5-7.

      - Brown, Salmon. 1914 communications and 1916 Interview with Fred Lockley, quoted in Bonnie Laughlin-Schultz, The Tie That Bound Us: The Women of John Brown's Family and The Legacy of Radical Abolitionism. New York: Cornell University Press, 2013.

   2. Secondary evidence comes from newspaper articles published during their travels which identify the family and pinpoint their locations. The following are just a few examples, in addition to **Attachment E**:

Evidence for the 1864 John Brown Family Camp Corral Sketch

- "The Brown Family." Gold Hill Daily News. September 29, 1864.
- "Wagon Trains!" Reese River Reveille. October 4, 1864.
- "Arrived." The Red Bluff Independent. October 6, 1864.
- "The Grave of John Brown." The Soldiers' Journal. October 5, 1864, 6.
- "World News." The Huddersfield Chronicle and West Yorkshire Advertiser. October 15, 1864, 10.

II. **The detailed mileage in Sarah Rousseau's diary places the Pella company in the exact same location as the Browns, as seen in her July 8, 9 & 10 written entries (See Attachment C):**

1. **July 8:** "Traveled this afternoon about 13 miles. 540 miles."

    Additional Support/Commentary – This count of 540 miles is a direct quote from the 1864 *Emigrant's Guide To Idaho* by John Lyle Campbell. In his guidebook, the 540 mileage marker is listed as "Road joins river. Wood, water and grass ….. 7 – 540." This mileage brings emigrants in proximity to the mouth of Sawmill Canyon in Glendo, Platte County, WY. **(See Attachments F & G)**

2. **July 9:** "…went about 3 or 4 miles when we came up with a train we had been in company with before … they had found good grass, and plenty of it … so here we have camped."

    Additional Support/Commentary – The mileage description brings the emigrants towards the Sand Draw basin, a slight detour off the main trail where they formed a corral with the Brown Train. **(See Attachment F)**

3. **July 10:** "Where we are camped we're surrounded by High bluffs. And sand for a carpet. … Started and came about 8 miles. To the right of the road we saw as we thought it at first to be a number of indian ponies, but it turned out to be emigrants … we turned in and camped there… We passed [crossed] Alder Creek this morning…"

    Additional Support – This day's ending mileage brings the Pella Company from Sand Draw back towards Sawmill Canyon, then northeast to the Alder Clump campsite. As counted in the 1864 *Emigrant's Guide To Idaho* by John Lyle Campbell, he includes: "Alder clump on left of road. Good place to camp ….. 9 – 549." **(See Attachment G)**

III. **The identity of the Brown Train is confirmed by multiple references specific to this encounter.**

1. **July 8**, Sarah Rousseau writes about the wagon train the Pella Company connected with, saying: "…it turned out to be the <u>New York Train</u> we had got acquainted with sometime back. They told us they had been laying over."

    Additional Support/Commentary– The Brown Train was emigrating from North Elba, New York and would likely be identifying themselves as being "from" New York, regardless of their brief winter stay from 1863-1864 in Decorah, Iowa. **(See Attachment C)**

2. **July 10**, Martha Roe writes about completing Sunday chores with Mary Brown at Alder Clump, saying: "After the usual work is don Mary [Brown] and I ascended one of those high mountains or legges [ledges] of rock…" **(See Attachment D)**

Additional Support/Commentary– Martha Roe names members of the Brown Train on ten specific occasions:

- Salmon Brown, Mr. Brown, Captain Brown: 7/8, 7/22, 8/6, 8/7, 8/13, 8/16
- Mrs. (Mary) Brown: 7/10, 7/13
- Miss (Annie) Brown: 7/13
- The children (Sarah & Ellen): 7/13

IV. **The written caption of the camp sketch supports the date of drawing (See Attachment A).**

Sarah Rousseau writes: "Camp by foothills up past the [*words illegible*] kenyin [*illegible*] on the 10th of July, 1864. Indians attack [*words illegible*] by this [*illegible*] miles from these Bluffs."

Additional Support/Commentary– The Pella Company, Roe Train, and Brown Train (combined) are exposed to a threat of Plains Indians attack on the evening of July 11, near Lost Creek (Glendo, WY). The Pella Company is attacked and robbed by Plains Indians in the afternoon on July 12, near Shawnee Creek (Orin, WY). The Brown Trains is assaulted by Plains Indians in the afternoon of July 13 near the Bozeman Trail (Douglas, WY). The Pella Company is attacked by Plains Indians in the afternoon of July 14 near the Bozeman Trail (Douglas, WY). These locations are within 25-60 miles from the camp depicted in the sketch.

My personal credibility to make this claim

I am a verifiable descendant of Sarah Rousseau, diarist of the source document and artist of the camp corral.

I have been researching and writing about the Pella Company's 1864 journey since 2014, beginning with preliminary work done with my uncle, Beverly Richard (Dick) Molony, the prior owner of the physical item being referenced **(See Attachments H & I)**. When he passed away in 2015, I continued researching the people and context of the trail diary with the assistance of and consultation with the following individuals:

- Mary Ann Anderson Strait, Granddaughter of Sarah Rousseau, via papers she has written **(See Attachment J).**
- Michael Molony, Son of Dick Molony.
- Pamela Greenwood, Verifiable descendant of the Curtis family who was also in the Pella Company **(See Attachment K)**.
- Stephen Daglish, Daglish Surname Historian & Descendant of Sarah Rousseau's uncle **(See Attachment L)**.
- Val Van Kooten, President of the Pella Historical Society.

Evidence for the 1864 John Brown Family Camp Corral Sketch

- Nicholas Cataldo, President of the San Bernardino Historical Society.
- Larry Cundall, Descendant-Owner of historical ranchland in Glendo, Wyoming near where this event occurred.

I have no reason to question Sarah Rousseau's mileage or descriptions of events.

Through the extensive research and preparation of the book *Emigrant Tales of the Platte River Raids*, I have found Sarah Rousseau's diary to have been corroborated by claims made by other wagon train members on the trail that same year. Of particular importance to this claim are the source records preserved in the following:

Earp, Nicholas. "Copy of a Handwritten Letter from Nicholas Earp to James Coplea," Pella Community Memory Database, Pella Public Library [Identifier: 2019.1.62.11], April 2, 1865.

Earp, Nicholas. "Copy of a Handwritten Letter from Nicholas Earp to James Coplea, April 2, 1865." Transcription by Janelle Molony and Nicholas Cataldo, November, 2023 in *Emigrant Tales of the Platte River Raids*, (Phoenix: M Press, 2023).

Roe, Martha A. *Guide to a Trip to Idaho, 1864,* Transcription by Harold Blinn. Manuscript at Washington State Univ. Library [Special Collections],1979.

Roe, Martha. *Diary of Martha Roe, May 4, 1864 to September 8, 1864, Grinnell, Iowa to Bannock, Montana.* Edited by Grace and Lester Burkett. Manuscript at Montana State Univ. Library [Special Collections], 1982.

Roorda, Gerrit. "Day Book of Gerrit E. Roorda, 1861 [sic, 1864]." Roorda Family History. Private publishing by William Frans Brunia, 1984, 37-34. (Copy held in Geisler Library Archives of Central College in Pella, IA.)

In Closing

Sarah Rousseau's sketch is an authentic image/representation of the Brown Train during their journey. In my opinion, these claims, which are backed by empirical evidence and compelling abductive reasoning, in addition to my personal relationship to and knowledge of the original artist offer unquestionable provenance to sustain any counter arguments or general disbelief.

Respectfully,

Janelle Molony
Official: JanelleMolony.com
Email: Janelle.Molony@yahoo.com

Evidence for the 1864 John Brown Family Camp Corral Sketch

Related Attachments

Attachment A – Item of Reference

Page Xa, on the opposite page from the back cover. Depiction of a camp corral. (Image Source: Courtesy of Dick Molony, Photographed by Nicholas Cataldo, 2015)

Page Xb, on the back cover. Depiction of bluffs. (Image Source: Courtesy of Dick Molony, Photographed by Nicholas Cataldo, 2015)

Evidence for the 1864 John Brown Family Camp Corral Sketch

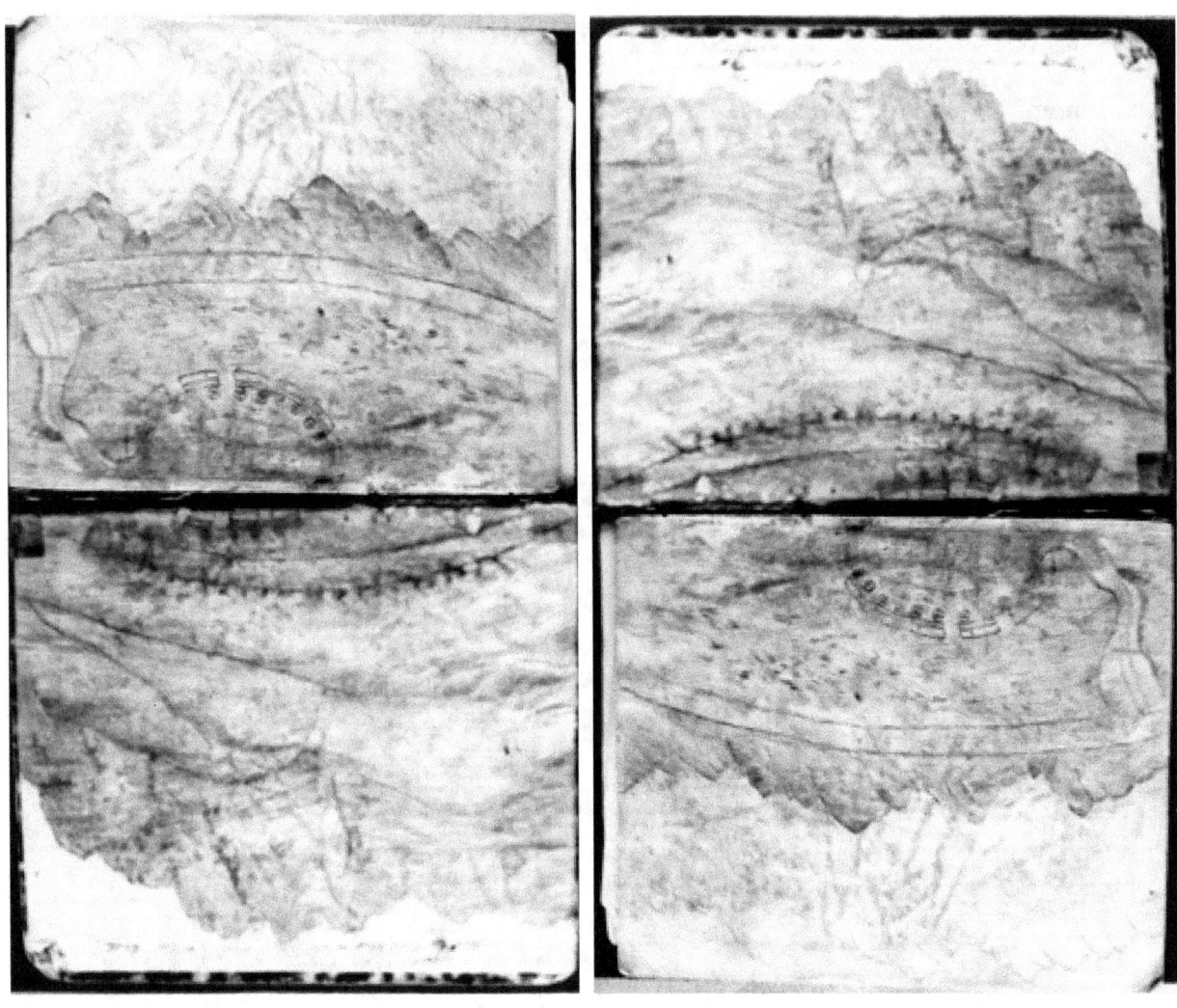

Alternative orientations of the images showing the complete 12-wagon circle.

Evidence for the 1864 John Brown Family Camp Corral Sketch

Second-to-last back cover page of Sarah Jane Rousseau's original 1864 diary, as photographed in 2015 by Nicholas Cataldo, President of the San Bernardino Historical Society. Photo enhancement and transcription by Janelle Molony, 3rd great-granddaughter of Mrs. Sarah Jane Rousseau, 02/08/2024.

1	2	3	4	5	6	7	8	9	10	11	12	13	14	15	16	17
Camp	by	foothills	up	past	the				kenyin	this	on	the	10th	of	July	1864
Indians	attack									by		miles	from	these	Bluffs	

I believe this transcription to be the most accurate based on visual inspection and through both personal and researched knowledge of the diarist and the historical, geographical, and contextual information that accompanies her story.

Signed & Dated _____ 2/8/24

Transcription of the written caption provided by Sarah Jane Rousseau.

Evidence for the 1864 John Brown Family Camp Corral Sketch

Attachment B – Wagon Train Rosters

Brown Train Roster

Party 1: From Decorah, IA, Vehicle Count = 1
Salmon Brown b.1836, Wagon Master, Son of John and Mary Brown
Abigail "Abbie" C. Hinckley Brown b.1839, Wife, Memoirist
Cora A. Brown b.1860, Child
Minnie Eliza Brown b.1863, Child

Party 2: From Decorah, IA, Vehicle Count = 1
Mary Ann Day Brown b.1816, Head of Household, Widow of John Brown
Anne "Annie" Brown b.1843, Child
Sarah Sadie Brown b.1846, Child
Ellen Brown b.1854, Child

Others: From Iowa, Vehicle Count = 1
George (NLN) b. N/A, Teamster/Driver
(NFN) Smith b. N/A, Teamster/Driver

Pella Company Roster (for the Month of July, 1864)

Party 1: From Pella, IA, Vehicle Count = 1
Nicholas Porter Earp b.1813, Wagon Master, Head of Household
Virginia Ann Cooksey Earp b. 1821, Wife
James Cooksey Earp b.1841, Child
Wyatt Barry Stapp Earp b.1848, Child
Morgan Seth Earp b.1851, Child
Warren Baxter Earp b.1855, Child
Adelia Douglas Earp b.1861, Child
Charles Lefterdy Copley b.1842 Teamster

Party 2: From Pella, IA, Vehicle Count = 2
Rev. Israel Coleman Curtis b.1813, Head of Household
Lucy Mildred Holman Curtis b.1819, Wife
Richard Henry Holman Curtis b.1843, Child
Emerine Holman Curtis b.1848, Child 1
Louis Foulk Curtis b.1852, Child
Allen Vail Curtis b.1855, Child
Israel Coleman Curtis Jr. b.1859, Child
Nancy E. "Lida" Curtis b.1861, Child
Penelope E. Curtis Born May, b.1864, Child

Party 3: From Pella, IA, Vehicle Count = 1
Stephen Thomas Hays b.1833, Head of Household
Mary Elizabeth "Eliza" Curtis Hays 1836, Wife

Party 4: From Pella, IA, Vehicle Count = 1
William Jesse Curtis b.1838, Head of Household
Frances Sophia Cowles Curtis b.1837, Wife
Holman Cowles Curtis b.1863, Child
Mack (unknown full name) b. N/A, Hired Teamster

Party 5: From Liberty, IA, Vehicle Count = 2
Dr. James Alexander Rousseau b.1812, Head of Household
Sarah Jane Daglish Rousseau b.1815, Wife, Diarist
Sarah Elizabeth Rousseau b.1849, Child
John James Rousseau b.1852, Child
John Albert Miller Rousseau b.1856, Child
Matilda Field b.1843, Aid to Sarah (Work-for-transport)
Thomas Jefferson ("TJ") Ellis b.1843, Hired Teamster, Wagon driver

Party 6: From Knoxville, IA, Vehicle Count = 1
John Bentley Hamilton b. abt. 1837, Head of Household
Sarah Jane Auten Hamilton b. abt. 1837, Wife
Oscar Hamilton b. Unknown, Non-biological son or ward
Baby Hamilton b. July, 1864, Child
Levi Tucker b.1833, Acquaintance from Knoxville

Party 7: From Navoo, IL, Vehicle Count = 1
William C. Clark b.1800, Head of Household
Mary Doyle Clark b.1804, Wife
Robert Pollack Parker b.1836, Captain/Guide, Son-in-law

Evidence for the 1864 John Brown Family Camp Corral Sketch

Attachment C – Excerpts from Sarah Jane Rousseau's diary

The 1864 Diary of Mrs. Sarah Jane Rousseau

May 13, 1864 to Dec. 18, 1864

Pella, Iowa to San Bernardino, California

Edited by Janelle Molony

The 1864 Diary of Mrs. Sarah Jane Rousseau

at present we are camped close by the river at an Indian Missionary Station.

Traveled 17 miles to-day. 510 miles Idaho territory July 6 1864.

Thursday 7th [July]

This morning cold enough for frost. We were not disturbed last night by the Indians. They appeared friendly. I suppose to-day will take us where there is more to be feared by them. We are now where there is plenty of wild currents[.] the first fruit we have seen. Our little boys went and got some yesterday evening, they are very large and the skin is tough on them.

The Indians here have rather a strange way of burying their dead. They have four sticks about 10 to 12 feet high and they placed their dead on top of them, it has a very singular appearance.

Having travelled about 6 miles this morning brought as opposite Ft. Laramie. The Dr. has gone across to Laramie to see if there is any letters for us. He has come back brought 2 letters with him.

Laramie has quite a picturesque appearance from this side. There is a good many Indians around. But we have not been disturbed by them.

Traveled 13 miles to-day. 522.

Friday 8 [July]

We came pretty near having an unpleasant time last night. We have to keep close watch day at night over the stock. Mr. Earp went to see about the

11

The 1864 Diary of Mrs. Sarah Jane Rousseau

was too dark to see. The poor horses was tired and hungry. We had a little meal that we mixed with some flour and water. Some would eat it and some would not so we corrreled, being as close together with possible, fastening the horses inside the Correle to the waggons and kept close guard all night. The wind still blowing very hard.

Traveled this afternoon about 13 miles. 540 miles.

Saturday 9th [July]

A pretty clear morning up quite early, harnessed up and started without breakfast and went about 3 or 4 miles when we came up with a train we had been in company with before.

We [didn't] know at first, but it might be the train the Indians had taken all their horses and left them a few days before, but it turned out to be the New York train we had got acquainted with some time back. They told us they had been laying over as they had found good grass, and plenty of it, and glad we were to hear it.

So here we have camped. While the stock are enjoying their bountiful repast. But the Indians are around. The men are guarding them. All well armed. The men have seen 5 or 6 of them, they are on horseback with their guns on their shoulders. We know they are hostile because they keep aloof.

Traveled between 3 or 4 miles to-day.

Sunday 10th [July]

A beautiful clear, still morning. Where we are camped we're surrounded by high Bluffs. And sand

The 1864 Diary of Mrs. Sarah Jane Rousseau

guards and he found they had got up a dance. And he told them they must quit their dancing and be on duty.

One of the soldiers told him to mind his own business and ordered him off. It made him awful mad and he was for killing. He used very profane language he could hardly be appeased. But he cooled down after a while and all was quiet.
This morning is pleasant and warm. Crossed Dry Creek. We are camped close by a blacksmith We have to stay and have some work done. We want to get away as soon as possible. The Blacksmith has a squaw for a wife. They are dreadfully low set. Started between 10 and 11 o'clock passed over some dreadful bad roads, rocky and broken. We had some very high hills to go over.

The scenery was grand, bordering on Romantic. One high hill towering above another in their majestic appearance. But worst of all was the wind, which blew a fair hurricane all the afternoon. The dust and sand almost putting our eyes out.

We had to keep pretty close together as the Indians are bad about stealing horses. There is a man that was about 100 yards behind the rest not thinking of danger when some Indians came from behind the Bluffs, and took his four mules out of his waggon and ran them off. He was too far from his train to get assistance. There is every opportunity to run them off, run them over the Bluffs and nobody could tell where they went.

Well we traveled until we got to the river[,] which was after sun down considerably. Watered our horses but could not find any feed for the stock as it

The 1864 Diary of Mrs. Sarah Jane Rousseau

for a carpet. There was nothing interrupted last night.

Started and came about 8 miles. To the right of the road we saw as we thought it at first a number of indian ponies, but it turned out to be emigrants, a great many of their company. We turned in and camped there ourselves as there was over 20 miles of bad mountainous roads and very poor prospect of getting good grass for our horses.

Here[,] there was plenty good grass and water and we did our washing[.] Sunday as it was. Oh it was a great deal against my feeling to have such things done but it seemed unavoidable. I hope e'r long we will get to the end of our journey.

Our trip has been made exceedingly unpleasant on account of Tom Ellis, his continued profanity whenever he was near. A more wicked man I never saw, and one more ungentlemanly. I believe he will leave this morning as Mattie won't do his washing anymore, he has treated her so unmanly cursing her all the time.

We passed Alder Creek this morning where there was [a] good spring[.] We watered our horses and got some for ourselves.

Travelled about 8 miles to-day.

Monday 11th [July]

A very pleasant morning, getting ready to make another start. Tom Ellis has gone with another family by the name of Clark. He got mad because Mattie would not do his washing. It has been the

The 1864 Diary of Mrs. Sarah Jane Rousseau

most pleasant day I have spent since I left home. We have heard no swearing. All has been quiet and pleasant.

The girls had to do the men's work. The doctor is pretty tired tonight. We must try and get someone else to go with us.

We have traveled over some rough roads to-day and we are now campt close to the River, a very pretty place. It is a pleasant evening, but quite windy.

Traveled to-day about 13 miles. 567 miles.

Tuesday 12th [July]

It is another pleasant morning. It is often when there is sorrow at night[,] "There is joy in the morning." It is even so with us at this time.

Last night after driving our horses across the river to feed[,] some one gave the alarm that Indians were around and that a gentleman in a train close by had just lost three of his horses[.] all that he had. He saw them cut the ropes they were fastened with and ran them off before they could get assistance. Well it caused a good deal of alarm.

They sent the word over the river to the guards that the Indians were about and they all commenced right away to gather up their teams to bring them back and form a correle and fasten the horses inside. The Dr.'s horses were all on the other side, consequently he had no horse to go after them. And he left them to those who were going after theirs to bring his[.] There being so many of them to bring, it

Evidence for the 1864 John Brown Family Camp Corral Sketch

Attachment D – Excerpts from Martha Roe's Diary

A TRIP TO IDAHO

(Edited by Harold E. Blinn)
6475 Nippy Canyon Road #135
Anmore Colo 80237

EDITOR'S NOTE: The following diary is a day-by-day record kept by Martha Ann Freeman Roe, who travelled with her husband Isaac Roe by wagon from Grinnell, Iowa to Bannack, Montana Territory in the summer of 1864. The diary was presented to the library of Washington State University by Mrs. Mary A. Burket of Spokane, Washington, a daughter of Mr. and Mrs. Isaac Roe, and is a part of the library's Western Collection.

Mrs. Roe entitled her account "A Trip to Idaho" since at the time she commenced her journey from Grinnell, Bannack was located in the Territory of Idaho. The Territory of Montana was established on May 26, 1864, and Bannack became the first Territorial capital. Mrs. Roe kept her account in pencil in a small notebook 6 inches by 7½ inches in size.

Isaac Roe was born in Lincolnshire, England in 1835 and came to the United States in 1858. After living in Grinnell, Iowa for three years, he travelled to Denver, Colorado Territory by ox

8 oclock and drove bout 9 M and camped for dinner had little better roads than we had the day before stopped bout 2 hours then started travailed 8 M in the afternoon and camped for the night bout 5 oclock got supper and went to bed

8 up this morning midling late on account of laying over we moved our waggons to a spring bout a mile from where we camped all day during the day Mr Cathcart and Mr Brown got a big dinner and I helped them after doing up the work I took a sleep when evening came there was bout 50 waggons camped with us making quite a little town then after taking a bite for supper we went to bed.

9 up this morning started in pretty good time travail till bout 2 p M and we turned out bout 1½h and got our dinners and the rest went on till they came to the river bout 5.P.M. we came bout an hour later I was sick all day with the Head ache after getting supper we went to bed

10 This is sabbath Morning we got up pretty late after the usual work is don Mary and I assended one of those high Mountains or legges of rock when we came back red the bible sung and went to the spring camped with some duck that swore awfully I baked bread then supper then chatted a while then prayrs then bed Alex still mad John and Sam went to a dance

Evidence for the 1864 John Brown Family Camp Corral Sketch

11 up this morning in pretty good time going to start early but the cattle being gon when we found them could not get them cross the river for more than an hour heard that we had to travail for 24 M without water but not so travailed bout 7 M and came to the river camped for noon then proceeded bout 6 or 7 M farther and came to the river where we caped for the night pretty good feed and water Alex wont drink milk

12 got up this morning little after sunrise started pretty good time drove bout 12 M and camped on the river bank under a large cotton wood tree started and drove bout 7 M and camped bout four oclock I washed a large washing on the bank of the Platt then got supper and went to bed

Indian attack

13 up this morning in pretty good time started and drove bout 9 or 10 M and camped on the river bank after going through some of the most mountainous countrie I ever saw Mrs and Miss Broun and I and children took a cutoff through the hills and mountains that shortened our road 3 or 4 M then came together at noon stopped bout 2 h and moved on bout 3 or 4 M and all calm the first thing we know a man came up and gave the alarm of an attack of the Indians ahead that we should hurrah up and get our fire armes for action we drove as fast as we could and drove on a huddle with the

Evidence for the 1864 John Brown Family Camp Corral Sketch

Attachment E – Additional Supports for the Brown Family Traveling in 1864

This ox-drawn covered wagon "stole the show" in Saratoga's first and finest 1912 pageant depicting the "History of California." Mr. S. P. Shorrocks in driver's seat and Miss Sarah Brown (right), youngest daughter of John Brown of Harper's Ferry, is wearing a replica of the calico dress and sun-bonnet she wore when crossing the plains by ox-team in the 1860's.

Image from *Saratoga's First Hundred Years,* by Florence Cunningham, 1967, p. 294

Attachment F - Google Earth Images of the Campsite Area

Wide View of Glendo, Wyoming showing from views of Sawmill Canyon to Alder Clump.

Closer View of South Fork Sand Draw, near where the campsite was situated.

Evidence for the 1864 John Brown Family Camp Corral Sketch

Attachment G – Excerpt from J. L. Campbell's Guidebook

EMIGRANT'S GUIDE TO IDAHO.		
Sand Hill Creek. South side of the road		1
Creek, or Slough	9—	397
Dry Creek. Thirty feet wide	5—	402
Crab Creek. Twenty feet wide; very shoal	4—	406

Two miles further you will find some high bluffs on the right. By ascending one of the highest, the visitor will see Chimney Rock to the west.

Small lake, south of road	2—	408
Cobb's Hills, west fort	8—	416

Party will find it sandy for ten miles.

Ancient Bluff runs north side of road, resembling the ruins of ancient castles	2—	418
Road joins the river,—good place to camp	11—	429
Low, sandy bluff, west fort	9—	438

The land for several miles is soft in wet weather, but good travelling in dry weather.

Chimney Rock, south side of river	14—	452

Here the land begins to be sandy and barren. Prickly pears and wild sage continue during the remainder of the journey.

Scott's Bluffs, south side of river	20—	472
Spring Creek, south side of road	4—	476
Road runs near the river,—good chance to camp	12—	488
Creek 200 yards south of road	5—	493

By ascending the highest bluff, a view can be got of Laramie Peak, in the Black Hills.

Timber north side of the river	11—	504
Raw Hide creek. Plenty of grass	6—	510
River opposite Fort Laramie	12—	522

FORT LARAMIE consists of both military and trading station. A good assortment of merchandise is kept here.

Dry Creek	4—	526
Good cold springs on right of road, near cottonwood trees	7—	533
Road joins river. Wood, water and grass	7—	540
Alder clump on left of road. Good place to camp	9—	549
For the next nine miles the road is somewhat sandy	9—	558
River. Good camping ground; wood, water and timber	9—	567
The road is now rough. After leaving the river four miles, the road descends to the river again	4—	571
Steep and craggy ascent. Road mountainous	10—	581
Road descends near the river. Sandy	5—	586
High, rolling, barren country for some distance. Low lands bordering upon the river	16—	602
Ferry of the Platte. Road rough	3—	605
Upper Platte ferry and ford	2—	607

Plenty of feed and some timber.

Road turns south and rises a long hill	7—	614
Mineral springs and lake. No bad taste to the water	6—	620
Rock avenue and deep descent	7—	627

The road here passes between high rocks, forming a kind of avenue or gate way, for a quarter of a mile.

Alkali swamps and springs. The party must avoid camping here. There is a creek north-west, in timber, and better grass	2—	629

Page 49 from J. L. Campbell's Emigrant Guide, 1864.

Evidence for the 1864 John Brown Family Camp Corral Sketch

Attachment H – Janelle Molony's Relationship to Sarah Rousseau

Janelle Molony's Family Lineage

James Alexander Rousseau (1813-1882)
Sarah Jane Daglish (1815-1872)

1. Mary Ann Rousseau (1843-1882)
2. Sarah Elizabeth Rousseau (1849-1931)
   (md.) Walter Percival Cave (1843-1898)

    a. William Lee Cave (1869-1919)
    b. Florence Evelyn Cave (1871-1947)
    c. Sarah "Jenny" Cave (1874-1935)
       (md.) Joseph Auther Molony (1871-1940)

        i. Joseph Arthur Molony Jr. (1909-1970)
        ii. Walter Beverly Molony (1898-1974)
            (md.) Marguerite Elenor Robertson (1904-1948)

            1. Beverly Richard Molony (1926-2015)
            2. Ronald Molony (1933-2011)
            3. Reginald Delbert Molony (1936-2019)

                a. Ryan Molony
                   (md.) **Janelle Molony**

    d. James John Cave (1876-1905)
    e. Walter Percival Cave (1881-1905)
    f. Daisy Mae Cave (1884-1948)
    g. Lester Percival Cave (1887-1918)

3. John James Rousseau (1852-1914)
4. Albert Miller Rousseau (1856-1920)

Evidence for the 1864 John Brown Family Camp Corral Sketch

Attachment I – Supporting Items from Richard (Dick) Molony

RICHARD MOLONY

January 14, 2003

Hanson: This is an interview with Richard Molony, January 14, 2003 with Joyce Hanson for the San Bernardino Oral History Project. Thank you for coming in. Let's talk about your grandparents and how they got to San Bernardino.

MOLONY: Well of course I'm not sure about my grandparents, we go back a generation before that. My great grandparents came from Iowa in a covered wagon in 1864 and settled in San Bernardino. They came basically for her health; he was a physician and a surveyor, a little bit of everything. But she had what apparently was rheumatoid arthritis and the weather in Iowa was such that-, and she was, she had married children by that time so I really don't know how old she was (I can go back and find it because I have her birth date)[Molony later verified her birth date was 1814], but they did come and settle here. Apparently first kind of up more in the Redlands area and then ended up in San Bernardino. My father was born in San Bernardino, and I don't know about-, I would assume, although I haven't checked the records that his mother, my grandmother, was also probably born in San Bernardino because the family was there. [Molony later added his grandmother was born in San Bernardino.] I was born in San Bernardino, but the hospital is no longer there, the Sequoia Hospital was down on the corner of Fifth and Arrowhead across from the post office. That post office was the main one at one time, it's no longer the main post office, but there's still a post office there. But I was raised more in Colton than I was in San Bernardino because my dad worked for the Southern Pacific Railroad, so we lived in Colton until the time of the depression when he was laid off for a while and we moved back to San Bernardino to live with my grandparents on my mother's side down on Mountain View between Fourth and Fifth. Then we moved back to Colton when I was in about the sixth grade, but always basically in this area.

Apparently the great grandparents who came, he was involved-, as a matter of fact I think he was County Superintendent of Schools at one time. He was also involved in Masonic work here, Rousseau was their name, R-o-u-s-s-e-a-u I think it is. And as far as I know there are no other direct descendents in this area. My father was one of two, and his brother never had any children, and we had the three boys, my two brothers and myself.

There's another Rousseau that lives up in the Bay area who I correspond with every now and then. We've never really met, but I've written back and forth with her and that sort of thing, but I never had a chance to meet her. She is more interested in the family and has traced it. Apparently the Rousseau's were active in Alaska with the territorial government and all that sort of thing. One of them I think was territorial governor at one time, but I don't' know that much about that side of the family. On my mother's side I don't know what the background is other than the state of Wisc has come up every now and then, so I'd assume that is the basic area, but when or where or u

Oral History interview of Richard (Dick) Molony for the San Bernardino Public Library's Oral History Project (January 14, 2003). https://www.sbpl.org/services/local_history/historical_treasures_of_san_bernardino/oral_history_project/richard_molony

Evidence for the 1864 John Brown Family Camp Corral Sketch

From: B Richard Molony <rmlm@sbcglobal.net>
To: Janelle.Molony <Janelle.molony@yahoo.com>
Date: Nov 23, 2014 at 10:38 PM

Hi Janelle and Ryan,
We too have a "todo" list which gets lost in the more mundane daily activities.
This week has been one of those. ML is an active member of the Community Hospital Auxiliary. I'm a member too but not as involved. I edit the newsletter, take pictures for the Historian, help ML whenever needed.
We just finished the Bazaar, and have taken a couple of trips to pickup goods to sell there. Now we're involved with holiday Auxiliary activities (warm clothes and food baskets.)
Thanks for the adopting process information. Let us know as progress is made.
I'm glad you're involved with genealogy. I tried when I retired but soon realized to really get into it takes a full time commitment. I'd rather spread my activities, so I joined the Camera club, took some classes, joined the SB Historical Society, and served on a couple of Boards at church.
The only family history activity we did was before I retired. We retraced the route of the wagon train that carried our roots to California.
In 1864 Dr. James and Sarah Rousseau left Knoxville, Iowa headed for better weather in California. She suffered with rheumatoid arthritis and was looking for a warmer climate.
That's why looking up Molony won't find you much. That's Dad's side of the family, which is too confusing to go into here.
My Grandmother Jenny was a Rousseau. Her side were the pioneers.
I'll attach a picture taken of four generations. I'm the kid in the sailor suit, the man is my Dad (also of course Reggie's), the two women are Jenny and her Mother who was part of the wagon train. I have the diary Jenny's Grandmother wrote while on the trip.
Try Googling "Sarah Rousseau's Diary."
I have gathered a bit of information. If you can't find anything on *Ancestry*, I'll send copies of what I have.
I'll also attach a new picture. Nine of us here went back to Mike and Karen's (Chris' folks) for the Balloon Fiesta. In the picture are the 14 from California. ML and me, our younger son, Rick and his wife Beckie, their daughter Katie, their son Matthew, his wife Katie Nicole, and their children, Landon, and Emmalyne. We sure had a good time; all in one motorhome.
Well, that's probably enough information to keep you busy for awhile. Email any questions.

Love, Uncle Richard

Sample correspondence between Richard (Dick) Molony and Janelle Molony from 2014.

Evidence for the 1864 John Brown Family Camp Corral Sketch

Attachment J – Supporting Items from Evelyn Anderson Straight (Granddaughter of Sarah Rousseau)

Anderson History I (excerpt/sample page), Evelyn-Anderson-Straight, Written for Marion County Daughters of the American Revolution, Published in the *Knoxville Journal Express* (August 30, 1934)

Evidence for the 1864 John Brown Family Camp Corral Sketch

Anderson History

Written for Marion County, Iowa DAR by Evelyn Anderson Strait (Condensed)
(It's Been A Honey, Part II Gen. p. 98, 104

James Rousseau, descended from Hillaire Rousseau who left his native land with thousands of other Huguenots and came to America in 1685.

James Rousseau married Sarah Jane Daglish in Safinaw, Michigan, and went to Wayne County, Kentucky, where the Rousseau family were living, and there on February 22, 1843, my mother, Mary Ann Rousseau, was born. Meanwhile, James Rousseau had graduated at the School of Medicine in Louisville and practiced there for awhile, but about 1845 moved with his wife and little daughter, Mary, first to Burlington, Iowa, and then to Elm Grove in Marion County, Iowa, near the place afterward called Lovilia, then a virgin forest, their nearest neighbor a mile away. The London-bred Sarah Jane told many amusing incidents of the rugged, primitive life. One, a country woman coming to call upon them and seeing the old-fashioned perforated tin cupboard on the back porch asked if that was the piano she had heard so much about.

In Iowa, my grandfather was again appointed United States Surveyor just as he had been in Michigan. Again he was given the work of mapping out a new country for those who would follow. The little town of Rousseau on the Des Moines River was named for him. He continued his practice of medicine here in old country doctor's style, making his visits on horseback, at times under great difficulties. I was told of one instance when his horse dropped dead after a long, hard, hurried ride to a patient.

Three other children were born in Elm Grove, and it was there that Jeff Anderson, teaching a country school and living about among the families of his pupils, saw Mary Rousseau, then twelve, and then and there decided he wanted to take her for his wife, which he did seven years later.

In 1763 there was born in Colchester, Connecticut, one Josiah Rogers Dodge who added his contribution to this sketch of the Anderson-Rousseau families. Dodge was a Baptist minister. Hardshell Baptists they were called, as were his descendants down and to including my grandmother (Lucinda Anderson). In 1775 or 1778 he became a member of Col. Chapman's regiment in Connecticut, and served throughout the revolution.

Following the close of the Revolutionary War, vast numbers of people from the New England states began migrating to the backland of Kentucky, the first state west of the Alleghany mountains to be admitted to the Union; and so when Josiah Rogers Dodge, married Zerirah Willis in Canterbury, Connecticut, in 1783, and took her a bride down the Ohio River to Kentucky, he made another step toward uniting these two families. It was the Anderson line now on its way to meet the Rousseau line. Elizabeth, a daughter of Josiah Rogers Dodge and Zerirah, was born in 1781 in Kentucky. In 1801 she married Samuel LaRue[2], and their daughter, Lucinda LaRue, born in 1802, married Robert Anderson in 1826 and they were my grandparents. The LaRues were mentioned in one

1. It's Been A Honey, Genealogy p. 109
2. It's Been A Honey, Genealogy p. 107, 108

Anderson History II (manuscript excerpt/sample page), Evelyn-Anderson-Straight, written for Marion County Daughters of the American Revolution, Published in the *Knoxville Journal Express* (ca. September, 1934)

Evidence for the 1864 John Brown Family Camp Corral Sketch

Attachment K – Supporting Items from Pamela Greenwood, Descendant of Israel & Lucy Curtis

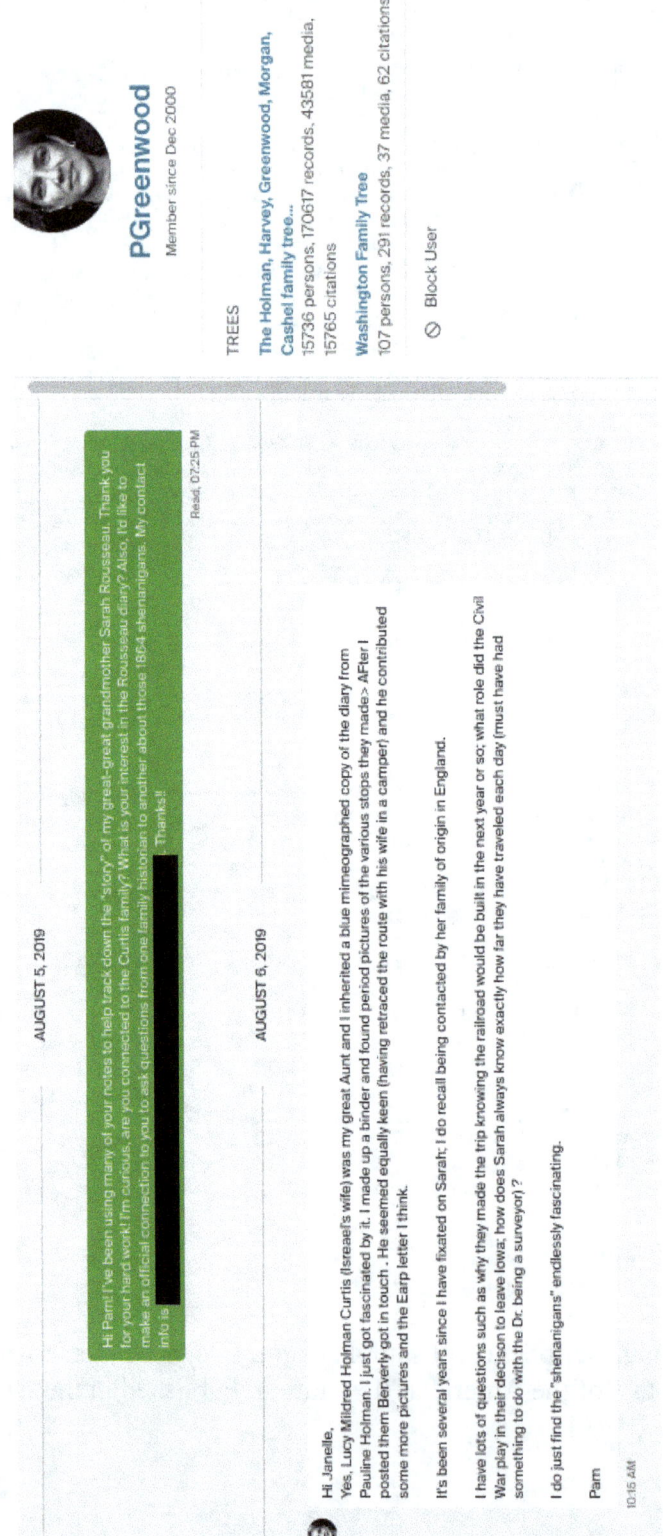

Sample correspondence between Janelle Molony and Pamela Greenwood (Ancestry.com, 2019).

News article that shows William Jesse Curtis retelling the stories of the wagon train journey for many years. "Relates Story of Early Days," *San Bernardino Sun*, (December 20, 1914).

Evidence for the 1864 John Brown Family Camp Corral Sketch

"CURTIS TELLS STORY While portions of the diary have been utilized for years by historians it remained for the Hon J. W. Curtis Sr., who owns a copy of the complete diary, to make it available for this article. ... **Efforts has been made to reproduce the account almost verbatim.***"*

News article that proves the son of William J. Curtis continued retelling the story of the wagon train journey. "Diary Tells of 1864 Trek by Covered Wagons," *San Bernardino Sun Telegram* (November 21, 1954).

Evidence for the 1864 John Brown Family Camp Corral Sketch

> Curtis, Wm. J. | February 25, 1965 San Bernardino's Free Press PAGE 9
>
> ## New school to be named in honor of pioneer resident W. J. Curtis
>
> The Wyatt Earp family served as "outriders" (guards) for the covered wagon train that brought William Jesse Curtis from Missouri to California as a young man. Curtis served as superintendent of San Bernardino County schools in the 1860's, and was at one time district attorney.
>
> Last week the school board decided to honor Curtis's memory by naming the new school at Sixth st. and Tippecanoe the William J. Curtis junior high school.
>
> Curtis's son, Jesse W. Curtis Sr., became a California Supreme court justice. His grandson Jesse W. Curtis Jr. is a former Superior court judge in San Bernardino and is now a federal district judge in Los Angeles.

News article that proves the role of the Curtis and Earp families on the wagon train journey. "New school to be named in honor of pioneer resident W. J. Curtis," *San Bernardino Free Press* (February 25, 1965).

Evidence for the 1864 John Brown Family Camp Corral Sketch

*"Jane never misses a day and is **remarkably factual in her reporting**." – Pamela Greenwood*

June 10, 2007 Pamela Greenwood (Descendant of the Curtis Family)

Commentary on Sarah Jane Daglish Rousseau's Diary

The four families (Rousseau, Earp, Hamilton and Curtis) started west from Knoxville, Marian County, Iowa on May 15, 1864. (Pella, site of the Curtis home, is also in Marian County.) They went due west from Iowa through Nebraska and Wyoming and then south through Utah, and a very small piece of Arizona, to San Bernardino, California. (Don't be confused by the Territories when you read the Diary.) This was known, from Iowa to Salt Lake City, as the Mormon Trail and then from Salt Lake City to San Bernardino as the Mormon Corridor. (San Bernardino had been a thriving Mormon community until it was abandoned by them when Brigham Young recalled his Saints to Salt Lake City in 1857.) They arrived in San Bernardino on December 17, 1864, a trip of seven months.

This was a well established and well used route and there appear to have been a number of other travelers on the road who intermittently join up with the Pella troupe and then separate, just as members of the Pella troupe themselves also separate and rejoin the caravan. It was a fairly loose operation, dependent on where they could find grass and water for their animals. Horses are mentioned most frequently although there is also mention of oxen and mules. They herded cows. Finding food for the animals was a constant problem. Sarah Jane is particularly fond of the horses who pull her "carriage" and all their horses have names.

They followed the telegraph lines and rivers (mainly the Platte and its tributaries) through much of Nebraska and Wyoming and there were "soldier stations" along the way. But these "stations" were poorly manned because of the Civil War and the group was plagued by Indians who were "not well controlled". During the first part of the journey these Indians were principally Sioux, Comanche, Arapahos, Snakes and Blackfoot and they posed quite a danger. During the later part of the trip, in Utah, the Indians were Piute and they were sometimes helpful -- but always made Jane Rousseau nervous.

During the latter half of the trip they frequently encountered Mormons, who were invariably friendly and hospitable. They even met Brigham Young and heard his brass band. Young had first settled the area in 1847 and by 1864 he had established friendly relations with the local Indians. In fact, Chief Kanosh (Jane calls him Canuse) had converted to the Mormon faith and had settled at Corn Creek (now Hatton in Millard County) with his band, where they were attempting to farm. Here the Pella band stopped for a month, from Sept. 22 to Oct. 20 and contracted with the Utes to care for their cattle!

Sarah Jane Daglish Rousseau makes note of several Mormon women from England. This is of particular significance because she herself had emigrated from London, England in 1833 and on page 72 she is amazed to find someone who knew her Uncle Thomas Elliott from New Castle on Tym, England. (Jane's mother was Mary Elliott Daglish.) Jane's personal history may account for her discriminating interest in the architectural trends she makes note of as she travels. Before her marriage Jane had taught music in Michigan and she was an accomplished pianist.

Frequent mention is made of letters to and from "Mary Ann". This was Jane's married daughter, Mary Ann Rousseau Anderson, who lived in Knoxville, Marion County, Iowa (the Diary's starting point) and at this time had one child, Eva Anderson, who was two. Mary Ann Rousseau had married Thomas Jefferson Anderson, a lawyer from Virginia, in 1862. She would have three more children and die in Knoxville in 1882. Jane may have written this diary in hopes that Mary Ann and her family would join the family in San Bernardino. It would have served as a good guide book.

The last part of the trip was clearly the most difficult and it appears the Mojave Desert almost did the Rousseau family in. There appears to have been dissension among the families on the trip at this point. The families again split up in an almost "every man for himself" way, and Lucy Holman Curtis was left to deliver her last child, Jennie, without Dr. Rousseau in attendance. However, she had other attendants who clearly were prepared to midwife her as Lucy's daughter, Mrs. Mary Curtis Hays, had herself recently delivered a son, Charles, just weeks before.

This was a harrowing seven month trip with three pregnant women and many small children, and an arthritic invalid (Jane) -- made during the last year of the Civil War. The Curtis family had been in Pella for twenty years and was well established. Israel was a state legislator, an attorney, Baptist minister and founder of Central University. He had nine children when the group started out and even his adult children went with him to San Bernardino. What could have precipitated this wholesale move?

One possible answer was the Conscription Act of February 1864, which had called all men between the ages of 17 and 50 to join the Union Army. Israel was just 50 in February 1864. And Israel was originally from Mississippi. He had two sons, William Jesse and Richard, who would have been eligible for this draft, and one son in law, Tom Hays. A Rousseau descendent, Dick Molony, says Nicholas Porter Earp, Wyatt's father, "had been in the Union Army at one time and was doing fine until Lincoln signed the Emancipation Proclamation (January 1, 1863). He was willing to fight to keep the union together, but not to free the slaves and resigned his commission and left."

(It is possible that it was these pro-Southern sympathies that may have precipitated Israel's move from Aurora, Indiana to Pella, Iowa in 1844. His wife's Holman family was strongly anti-slavery even at that early date --as early as 1829 Jesse Lynch Holman had been a founder of the American Colonization Society, organized to send freed slaves back to Africa.)

N. P. Earp, the nominal leader of the group, had lived in Pella for about 20 years and had had a 160 acre farm there. He had been to San Bernardino before and liked the look of it. But N.P. had a checkered past with bootlegging and problems with the law (mostly for non-payment of debt.) And he was peripatetic. By 1870 he and his entire family are in Lamar, Barton County, Missouri. By 1880 they

Personal essay about the Pella Company wagon train experience from Pamela Greenwood (June 10, 2007). Originally shared on Geni.com, see https://www.geni.com/people/Sarah-Rousseau/6000000002726007533 and republished with illustrations at https://janellemolony.com/2023/09/descendant-weighs-in

Evidence for the 1864 John Brown Family Camp Corral Sketch

are back in San Bernardino, this time in Temescal. One only hopes that the family's second trip was made on the newly completed transcontinental railroad. N.P. Earp is the most problematic person on the trip, from Jane's point of view.

Wyatt Earp was sixteen when he made this trip. In later years he claimed to have provided Buffalo meat to the wagon train with his first gun, which his father had given him before their start. Jane does not appear to have received any of Wyatt's largess. Also on the trip was Wyatt's older brother, James C. Earp. At 23 James had served in the 17 Illinois infantry, Company F and had lost the use of his left arm at Fredericktown, Missouri, on October 8, 1862. He left the train at Austin, Nevada. Morgan S. Earp was thirteen, Warren B. Earp nine and Delia Earp just three.

Comparing this Diary to those discussed in Women's Diaries of the Westward Journey by Lillian Schlissel, one is struck by the uniqueness of Jane's situation. First, she is invalided and thus spared much of the daily drudge of chores discussed by many. She says she was "almost useless" at the beginning of the trip and by the end she says she "can help a little."

Jane is meticulous in counting each day's mileage. Twenty five miles is a good day. (One assumes the trail is somehow marked by 1864.) Jane never misses a day, and is remarkably factual in her reporting. She notes earthquake activity, volcanic activity, and problems with quick sand in the rivers. Like other women she is knowledgeable about which grasses are best for the stock animals.

Group dynamics are rarely discussed, except towards the end of the trip when there is clearly tension. But there are indications of this tension as early as July 29 when Jane says, "From some cause, we cannot define, (among) some of those we thought our true friends there appears to be hard feelings, and jealousy existing, whether it is from false tales told around the camp or not I cannot tell. It is one of the best kinds of places for such things." Visiting back and forth seems to have been infrequent. I would guess the other women on the train were extremely busy. There were more children on this train than was usual and their over all numbers were small.

The one person Jane singles out for particular attention is Mattie Field, apparently a young woman who is paying to travel with her family. She helps with chores but is sick several times during the early part of the trip, and she becomes very indecisive by the time they reach Salt Lake City. (Mattie's departure means 14 year old Elizabeth/Libby now must do most of the cooking and laundry.) And Mattie does have a mysterious end...

On the other hand, the loss of Tom Ellis does not seem to carry the same impact on Jane, who does not miss his offensive language. Apparently hired to assist fifty one year old Dr. Rousseau, Tom is not replaced until November when Charley Copley joins the family. He has joined them just in time to make a heroic rescue mission in the Mojave Desert. He and Richard Curtis walk through the desert to bring relief to the stranded Rousseaus.

The early incident with young Allen Curtis when he fell from the mule wagon and it ran over him was a very common occurrence with young children and what is remarkable is that he "got well". Many children died as a result of such accidents and they seem to have been frequent.

Counting graves was common. Having no deaths on the trail was uncommon and may be a testament to Dr. James Rousseau's skill as a physician. (His patients seem always to recover. Jane also expresses confidence in his healing powers with horses.) In general, accidents and illness were a more common cause of death than were Indian raids. In fact, Indian raids were relatively uncommon.

Noting the weather conditions and the passing scenery are in every diary written by women on these trips. However not many travelers had a "marine glass" for their amusement and safety. Undoubtedly the Rousseau's have this piece of equipment because Dr. Rousseau had previously been a government surveyor. A fair day and a fine scene were greatly to be wished for. Rain was helpful with laying the dust, but wind was a problem because it could cause the wagons to over turn and hail of course could tear the canvas. Snow made the trail hard to follow and was particularly difficult for the draft animals, as was sand.

A modern reader is struck with the delicacy Jane uses in describing childbirth. One day Mrs. Hayes is "sick" and the next day she mysteriously has a new baby. Same with Mrs. Hamilton and Mrs. Curtis. ..

The September 1857 Mountain Meadows Massacre, noted on page 79, is a well documented event in which a Mormon militia and some Paiute Indians killed an entire wagon train of Arkansas farming families known as the Baker/Fancher party, traveling from Arkansas to California. Around 120 unarmed men, women and children were killed. Seventeen younger children (none older than six) were kidnapped and cared for by local Mormon families and eventually returned to their relatives. In 1859 Brevet Major James H. Carleton, commanding some eighty soldiers of the First Dragoons from Fort Tejon, California, had erected a stone cairn at the site. The stone cairn was topped with a cedar cross and a small granite marker was set against the north side of the cairn and dated 20 May 1859. There have been a number of subsequent monuments erected and John D. Lee, the Mormon militia leader, was executed after several trials.

The Massacre was a unique episode in Mormon history. Seven years later the Mormons Jane writes about are almost universally helpful. All of the Mormons had made the same trip our little band was making and they were experienced with the hardships. One assumes their experinces had been instrumental in the Pella groups preparations for the trip. The following information would have informed their preparations.

"The Mormon leaders recommended, in fact insisted, each Mormon family of five members take with them the following: One good strong wagon, provided with a light box; two or three good yoke of oxen between the ages of 4 and 10 years; three or more good milk cows; and one or more beef animals; three sheep, if they could be obtained; 1,000 pounds of flour or other bread stuffs in good

Personal essay about the Pella Company wagon train experience from Pamela Greenwood (June 10, 2007). Continued.

Evidence for the 1864 John Brown Family Camp Corral Sketch

sacks; a working rifle or musket for each male over 12 years old; one pound of gunpowder; 4 pounds of lead; 1 pound of tea; 5 pounds of coffee; 100 pounds of sugar; 1/2 pound of cayenne pepper; 2 pounds of black pepper; 2 pounds of mustard; 10 pounds of rice; 1 pound of cinnamon; 3/4 pound of cloves; 1 dozen nutmegs; 25 pounds of salt; 5 pounds of saluterious; 10 pounds of dried apples; 1 peck dried beans; a few pounds of bacon or dried beef; 5 pounds dried peaches; 25 pounds of seed grain; 1/2 gallon alcohol; 20 lbs of soap; 4-5 fish hooks; 15 lb.. of iron and steel; a few pounds of wrought nails; one or more saws and grist mill cranks; 2 sets of pulley blocks per wagon; a coil of rope to fit blocks; a fish seine and hook; 25 to100 pounds of farming tools or mechanical tools; cooking utensils were to be; a bake kettle, frying pan, coffee pot, teakettle and cups, plates, knives, forks, spoons and other pans, the fewer the better; a good tent to be used by 2 families; clothing and bedding for each family not to exceed 500 pounds. "At the end of the list was the notation, horses or mules could be substituted for ox teams.

"The approximate weight of a wagon load was a little over one ton." (Taken from a news article written by Ralph Arnold)

Date: 1864

Place: Knoxville, Iowa to San Bernardino, California

Description: Wagon train trip with Israel Coleman Curtis family

PGreenwood originally shared this on 10 Jun 2007

Personal essay about the Pella Company wagon train experience from Pamela Greenwood (June 10, 2007). Continued.

Evidence for the 1864 John Brown Family Camp Corral Sketch

Attachment L – Supporting Items from Stephen Daglish, Relative-Descendant of William Daglish (Sarah Jane Daglish Rousseau's father)

On Fri, Mar 23, 2018 at 3:52 PM, Stephen Daglish wrote:

PM   Yahoo Mail - Re: Family member looking for a copy of Sarah Daglish/Rousseau's Diary

> Dear Janelle,
>
> Thank you so much for your email - it is great to hear from you. I am very sorry to hear that Richard (Dick) Molony has passed away.
>
> I am away at a genealogy conference in the UK this weekend (the Guild of One-Name Studies, whose members study surnames) and will be back home on Monday.
>
> I have a hard copy of the diary, so perhaps will need to scan this to send to you. I can check what else I have - I think it came with some correspondence.
>
> I will get back to you on Monday when I am home.
>
> Thanks again.
> With best wishes,
> Stephen Daglish
>
> Sent from my iPad
>
> On 23 Mar 2018, at 20:45, Janelle Decker Molony wrote:
>
>> Hello! I'm glad I found your blog about Sarah Daglish / Rousseau (http://daglishfamily.blogspot.com/2007/06/sarah-jane-daglish-trip-across-plains.html). I'm married to Ryan Molony, the great-great-great grandson of hers. Our uncle, RIchard Molony (You called him Dick Molony in your blog post), was the family historian who volunteered at the San Bern. Historical Society... and gifted them the diary. He has since passed and we are trying to get a copy of the item somehow. Would you be willing to work with me to get a copy of the transcription? I've sent a request to the historical society as well.
>> I've attached a copy of an e-mail my uncle sent to me regarding his involvement with the society and Sarah's story to corroborate my story and request. I can also send you some of the items I have collected regarding her descendants and photos you may or may not already have.
>>
>> Respectfully,
>>
>> - Janelle Decker Molony (In ▇▇▇ with the Molony "clan.")
>
> <email from richard molony copy.pdf>

Sample correspondence between Janelle Molony and Stephen (2018).

Evidence for the 1864 John Brown Family Camp Corral Sketch

The Daglish Family

For anyone interested in the Daglish name - includes things that I have found in my research and stories about the name

SATURDAY 9 JUNE 2007

Sarah Jane Daglish - Trip Across The Plains

This week I received a transcribed copy of a remarkable diary written about a journey across the plains of the United States from Knoxville, Iowa to San Bernardino, California. It was written by Sarah Jane Rousseau (nee Daglish). Below is a page from the original diary.

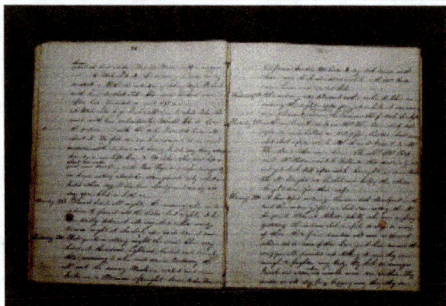

The story begins in England in North Shields, Northumberland, where William Daglish (who is my g-g-great uncle) married Mary Elliott in May 1812 at Christ Church, Tynemouth. The couple had two daughters, Mary Ann and Sarah Jane. In the 1820s the family moved to London, from where they emigrated to the United States, arriving in New York in 1833.

A picture of family life in London is given in an article written by Sarah's granddaughter Evelyn Anderson-Strait. She wrote that the family lived in Brunswick Square where the girls were taught by tutors "and for seven years they were taught by a music master who had been a pupil of Beethoven".

In America, Sarah met James Rousseau, who had been sent on a government mission to survey the then unknown lands of Michigan. He later became a doctor, and the couple married in 1839, having 4 children. There is a a pair of portraits of Sarah and James, which are reputed to have been painted by Samuel Morse, inventor of Morse code - but otherwise a distinguished portrait painter.

In 1864 the Rousseaus (Sarah, James, and children Elizabeth, John and Albert - elder daughter Mary Ann stayed behind in Iowa) joined three other families in a wagon train to San Bernardino. The others were the Earp, Hamilton and Curtis families. The Earp family included the notorious Wyatt Earp, then 16 years old.

It was a hazardous journey, setting out in May and arriving in December, seven months later. The reason for the Rousseaus making this trip seems to have been for Sarah's health; at this time she was crippled by arthritis and she believed the warmer climate would give some relief.

Their route followed the so-called "Mormon Trail" to Salt Lake City, and then the "Mormon Corridor" to San Bernardino. Although established routes, there were still hardships and dangers, particularly from Indians.

About Me

Stephen Daglish
My name is Stephen Daglish. I have an interest in genealogy and local history. For several years I have run the Daglish and Dalgleish One-Name Studies which look at the history of the name and those who hold or have held the name. More recently I have started a study of Great and Little Kimble in Buckinghamshire where my maternal ancestors, the Rutlands, lived.

View my complete profile

Visitors:
64281

Blog Archive
- ► 2016 (1)
- ► 2011 (2)
- ► 2009 (5)
- ► 2008 (23)
- ▼ 2007 (58)
  - ► December (7)
  - ► November (6)
  - ► October (4)
  - ► September (3)
  - ► August (3)
  - ► July (7)
  - ▼ June (6)
    - The Daglish clockmakers of Alnwick
    - Ian Daglish, military historian
    - Jenny Hay, contemporary sculpture
    - Ben Daglish, musician and composer
    - Sarah Jane Daglish - Trip Across The Plains
    - Eric Fitch Daglish, author and engraver
  - ► May (5)

Stephen Daglish's research into the Diary with the help of Dick Molony and Pamela Greenwood (2007), https://daglishfamily.blogspot.com/2007/06/sarah-jane-daglish-trip-across-plains.html

Evidence for the 1864 John Brown Family Camp Corral Sketch

Evidence and Items of Provenance from Nicholas R. Cataldo

Personal contact information has been reduced or entirely redacted from this public document.

2/8/2024

Provenance Claim Re: Details found in the 1864 Diary of Sarah Jane Rousseau, San Bernardino Pioneer Resident

To whom it may concern:

I have been researching the legendary Earp family for almost 40 years and have written extensively on their history, including the 1864 journey across the Great Plains that was documented in a diary kept by Sarah Jane Rousseau.

This diary belonged to the late Richard Molony of San Bernardino, Ca., whom I personally knew and can vouch for as a descendant of the diarist.

I've personally held and inspected the physical item being reviewed and wholly agree that this item is from the original 1864 diary of Mrs. Sarah Jane Rousseau and the sketches are located along with hand-written contents. I have read portions of the original diary, typed excerpts and various transcriptions and can verify that Sarah Rousseau's claims about her travel whereabouts are consistent and trustworthy. I have no reason to believe she would fabricate any details in her sketch.

I have also read the original (copy) and several transcribed copies of the 1865 letter from Nicholas Earp retelling his story about the journey to James Copla and agree that Earp's letter corroborates Sarah's claims about dates, events and locations without question.

If you have any questions, do not hesitate in contacting me.

Respectfully,

[signature: Nicholas R. Cataldo]

Nicholas R. Cataldo

San Bernardino Historical and Pioneer Society

President

Yankeenut15@gmail.com

Evidence for the 1864 John Brown Family Camp Corral Sketch

Related Attachments

Attachment A – Sample images of the 1864 Diary of Mrs. Sarah Rousseau, photographed by Nicholas R. Cataldo in 2015, with the permission of MaryLou Molony (1930-2016) of Redlands, California.

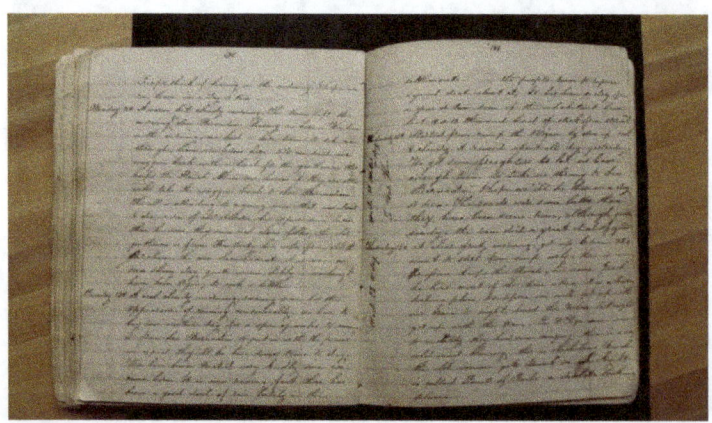

Sarah Rousseau's 1864 Diary, Molony Family Collection, photographed by Nicholas R. Cataldo, 2015. All Rights Reserved.

Evidence for the 1864 John Brown Family Camp Corral Sketch

Sarah Rousseau's 1864 Diary, Molony Family Collection, photographed by Nicholas R. Cataldo, 2015. All Rights Reserved.

Evidence for the 1864 John Brown Family Camp Corral Sketch

Attachment B – Image of Beverly Richard Molony (left, 1926-2015) with Nicholas R. Cataldo (right).

Richard was the owner of the original item and prior had shown it to Nicholas Cataldo as a possible donation to the San Bernardino Historical and Pioneer Society.

Attachment C – Image of Beverly Richard Molony (front, almost age 4).

Richard is posed with Mrs. Sarah Elizabeth Rousseau Cave (daughter of Sarah Jane Rousseau), Mrs. Marguerite R. Molony and Walter Beverly Molony (Richard's parents). March 6, 1929, courtesy of Richard Molony (Molony Family Collection).

Evidence for the 1864 John Brown Family Camp Corral Sketch

Attachment D – Evidence of Easily Accessible Material to Corroborate the Subject Material

Letter from Nicholas Earp to "James Coplea," April 1865. Held at the Pella Public Library.

Evidence for the 1864 John Brown Family Camp Corral Sketch

STORIES OF INDIANS TOLD BY N. P EARP

The Pella Chronicle, April 28, 1938

C. Hospers of Orange City Sends Chronicle Letter Of Interest

MARSHALL OF THIS CITY

Earp Was City Councilman In 1861 and Marshall 1862 to 1864

The Chronicle has received from C. Hospers of Orange City a letter written in April 1865 by N. P. Earp to one James Copla, telling of experiences with Indians and detailing other incidents of those days. The letter came into the possession of Dr. Thaen of Orange City, and Mr. Hospers knowing of it, thought it might be of interest to our readers.

Mr. Earp and others of the family were well known here, where he was a member of the city council in 1861 and from 1862 to 1864 was city marshall. He resigned in April of the latter year, and this was probably near the time that he went west. He was much in the forefront at the outbreak of the Civil war, and it is said that he would gather men around him at Cox's tavern, on the site of the Marion County State bank and talk to them regarding the matter. The Earp home was on the site of the Geo. Stout residence on the northwest corner of West Market.

The following letter has been typed, preserving the original style of the writer, with the spelling and punctuation (or lack of it) unchanged, just as Mr. Earp wrote it. It is as follows:

April 2nd 1865

James Copla
Dear Sir

After a long elapse of time and agreate deel of anxiety waiting for a letter from you in answer to one I wrote to you from Corn Creek Utah Teritory and finding out from Charleys letter that he just received from you that you had not received any from me.

I embrace the presant opertunity of wrighting you another letter to let you know how it is with me and family and all the friends myself and family are all well as are all the friends that came across the plains with me. and we hope these fuw indifferant written lines may find you all well when they come to hand together with all enquiring friends now James as you did not get my other letter that I rote to you in which I had given you a full account of our trip and the incidents thare, to as fair as Corn Creek Utah Teritory 171 miles south of Salt Lake I will endeavor to give you a slite history of the trip through. and some of the occurancys that took place on the trip but cannot give it in full detail for two mutch time has elapsed for me to remember all suficient to do so and it would take more time and paper than I have to spare at this time but will try to satisfy your mind to some extent and the many others that I know are ancious to beare from us.

Mule Wagon Ran Over Him

Well here we go across the Missouri river as you know. we had to do to cross the plains just before we got to the river at the Crossing place little Allen Curtis fell from the mule waggon and it ran over him and came verry near killing him but we crossed over and the boy got well and on we went. with tolerble good luck and speed considering the scerceness of grass for our animills untell we got to Ft. Larimie which we did on the Seventh day of July just one month and seven days from the time we crossed the Missouri River.

And on we went without any serious trouble occasionally passing indians on the rout untill we got about 50 miles above Larimie we began to hear of depradations being counted by the Indians on trains but we not seeing any of it and it was reported always behind or before us and as we did not see any of the occurancys the crowd began to think that it was all false and as they had bin before pretty mutch all the way or at least some of them a little to slack in doing thier duty when in camp in garding the stock they began to be still more so until I began to scold some about it and told them that we would have to have a demstration from the Indians which I believed would take place before long and I would not care mutch if we did so so they did not hurt any of us as I thought it would be the cause of them being more prompt in doing thir duty and cause them to see the necessity of more care and vigelance.

Grass Is Scarce

And shure anough when about 50 miles above Larimie one day when in camp for noon in the bend of Platt River the grass being verry pore on the side that we war campt on I rode across the river and found that on the other side that thare was good grass so I gave the order for the stock to be turned over the river my hands took my horses and all the cattle over the ballance turned some of thirn over sutch as they could drive over after the rest but some would not go over and some said they would rather thirn would stay on the side they war on than to put them into the river.

I gave orders to those that went across the river that in case I gave the alarm to git hold of thir horses picket rops as quick as possible and bring them across the river into camp Some had bin in camp but a little while, I. B. Hamilton I C Curtis Dr. Rusau and myself were seated on the bank of the river talking and I happened to look around behind me and about four hundred yards off I saw a squad of men on horse back galoping towards us I sprang to my feet and sang out indians to arms boys and we all rushed to the waggons and got our guns and ran to meet the red skins who by this time was amonst the horses that war on our side of the river hooping and yelling like indians shure enough.

Clash with Indians

We met them and began to shoot at them and we soon checked them up and turned them back while one of them was in the act of trying to lasoe one of Hamiltons mares I leveled the rifle I got of Grafe at him and at the crack of the gun he fell forward in his saddle and turned his horse round and ran off badly wounded I am shure. but the yells of the savages and the firing of the guns fritened our horses so that it caused them to stampeed and ran down apast the Camp.

In spite of all that we could do they took back down the road the indians seeing that ran round and got in between us and the horses and ran them off at the commencement of the fun according to directions I hollowed for the stock on the other side to be brought over and as soon as it could be got over I took ten men and persued them until dark but with out effect the conciquence was they got ten head of our horses 5 of Hamiltons 4 of Rusaus and one of Curtises next morning on we went and the second day after they had made the first raid on us we camped again for noon in abend of Platte River situated a good deal as before only we had all our stock on the same side of the river that the waggons was on. and we had our gards properly posted and pickets out for it was no trouble now to get the men all to do their duty.

Meet Indians Again

We had not bin in camp long untell the Sentinels gave the alarm that the Indians was comming so I ordered the horses to be brought inside the corell by the gards that was garding them the women all turned out to help get the horses into the corell while we who was not on gard gethered our guns and rushed to meet the Indians when they got as closet as we entended them to come we comenced poping away at them and soon succeeded in checking them and puting them to flite they ran off about a half a mile and stoped and turned round as tho they war not satisfied.

I said boys they are not satisfied lets satisfy them so I ran to the waggons and gumped upon a horse and said we'll make them leave there. Dr. Rusau T. J. Ellis James Earp and a young man by name of Tucker that was with Hamiltons and two other men that got in with us followed suit and off we charged after the Indians when they saw we war making for them they wheeled about and off they put. on we went in full persuit of them untell they found were about to over take them then faced about to gave us battle they were about 4 to one of us I gave orders to form a line of battle and we went into a general engagement they undertook to flank us first to the right and then to the left. but they found out they couldn't for they had their match.

Flying of Arrows

So they then began to give back the arrows flew and the bullets whised they began to gave back to keep out of range of our guns we rushed on when Dr. Rusau put his mareen glasses to his eyes and descovered the man who seemed to be leading the band gaving comand was a white man he hollowed out Earp shoot that man on the roan horse he is a white man as I was closest to them I leveled jon him and at the crack of the gun he fell to one side of the horse but caught in the mane and recovered again then wheeled his horse and lumbered over the hill as fast as his horse would take him the rest immediately took to flight following him we had exhausted all our shots.

So we had to stop the persuit but saw by the blood on the trails that we had woonded 4 of them so that was the last time we was attacked by the Indians the next morning we started on a gain nothing of any consequence hapning from that to Salt Lake only Mrs. Hamilton brought forth a fine boy a few days after we were attacked by the Indians we got to Salt Lake on the 12th day of August when we ought ta have bin thare by the first.

Hot Sands of Desert

Then we ascertained by the old Salt Lake frieghters that we could not go to California on the southern rout untill about november on account of having to cross the Great American desart becaus it would be to hot before that time to cross it so we lay by nine weeks waiting for the wether to get coal anough and at the proper time we took up the line of Martch again and on the 20th day of December we landed in San Barnardina after a long and tedious trip I got through with all the stock I started with but one mares died at Utah Lake with the collic.

Comparitively in good order my blind horse at the bever dam two hundred miles from San Barnardino fell down abank about fifteen fet high and disabled himself so that I had to leave him non for what am doing I succeeded in renting afine farm the 3rd day after I got to San Barnardino and on the 25th day moved out to it about 10 miles from San Barnardino it has ten acres in peach and apple ortchard and 35 acres in grapes. Oh don't you wish you and many others of my friends was here to help me eat apples, peaches and grapes this fall & drink wine I got here a month to late to get in large a crop as I wanted to.

Vegetables All Winter

The people was most done sowing when I got on my farm I have 12 acres in wheat 18 in barley which is now in the boot & I have 20 acres now planted in corn ten of which is large anough to plow and shall plant 8 more this week then I shall be done planting, letis large anough to east of our own swoing but we have had lettis & cabage all winter which was growing here when we came we have our peas stuck and onions large anough to eat of our own planting I set out 20 lbs. of onion sets and about a quarter of an acre in onion seeds my potatoes is large anough to work, peaches as large as small birds eggs.

This is the finest climate in the world altho I don't know that I shall stay here and think I shall not for I did not start from home expecting to stop here but when we got heare we ware all so near run through that we could not go longer I no of places in California that I like better than I do here but if a man has got hom a place after the first year he can live as easy as any place in the world and as pleasant but I expect to go higher up in California or into Arisonia or to some one or the other.

"Stories of Indians Told By N. P. Earp," *The Pella Chronicle*, (April 28, 1938)

Evidence for the 1864 John Brown Family Camp Corral Sketch

Attachment E – Evidence of Nicholas R. Cataldo's Body of Work Specific to the Subject

The Earp Clan: The Southern California Years (2006, Backroads Press).

"Sarah Jane Rousseau: Diary of the Earp Wagon Train to San Bernardino," City of San Bernardino, 1999). https://www.sbcity.org/about/history/pioneer_women/sarah_jane_rousseau

"This pioneer's cross-country trip to San Bernardino," San Bernardino Sun (March 21, 2022). https://www.sbsun.com/2022/03/21/pioneer-sarah-jane-rousseaus-diary-offers-details-of-cross-country-trip-to-san-bernardino/

"San Bernardino's lush valley, Nicholas Earp's attitude detailed in early pioneer's diary," San Bernardino sun (April 18, 2022). tps://www.sbsun.com/2022/04/18/san-bernardinos-lush-valley-nicholas-earps-attitude-detailed-in-early-pioneers-diary/

Evidence for the 1864 John Brown Family Camp Corral Sketch

"Stories of survival from perilous 1864 wagon trek to San Bernardino," *San Bernardino Sun* (January 22, 2024). https://www.pressenterprise.com/2024/01/22/stories-of-survival-from-perilous-1864-wagon-trek-to-san-bernardino/

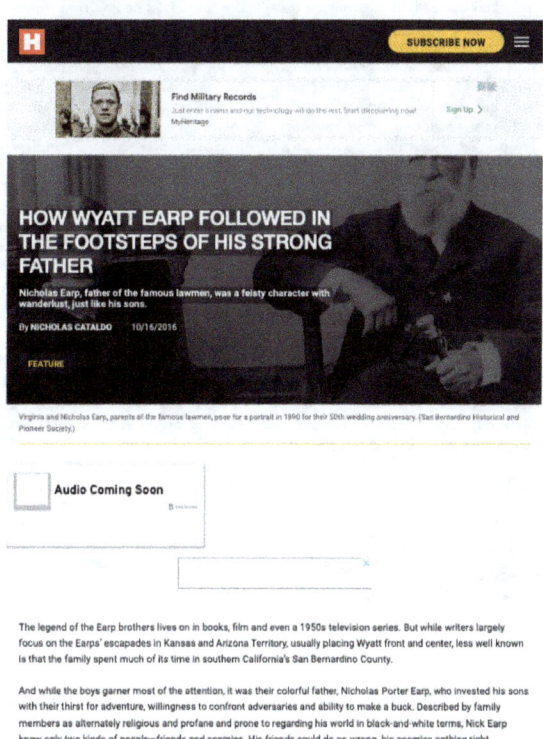

How Wyatt Earp Followed in the Footsteps of his Strong Father," HistoryNet (October 16, 2016). https://www.historynet.com/nicholas-earp/

Evidence for the 1864 John Brown Family Camp Corral Sketch

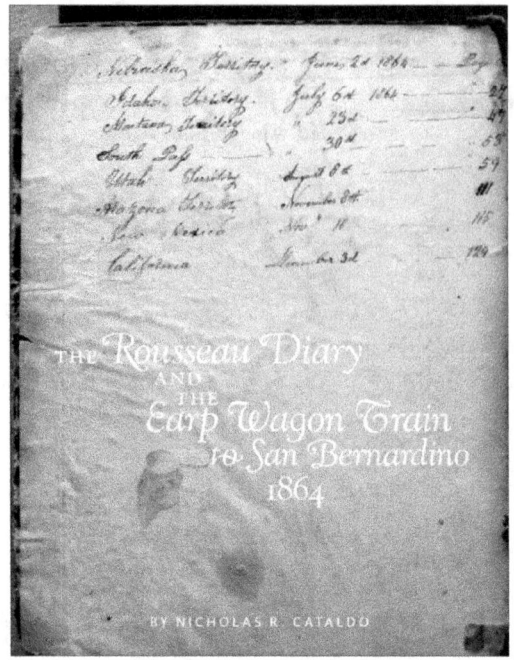

ABRAHAM LINCOLN'S EMANCIPATION PROCLAMATION WENT INTO EFFECT ON JANUARY 1, 1863, WAVES OF JOY AND CELEBRATION TOUCHED MANY AMERICANS, both black and white. However, not everyone was happy with this presidential announcement granting freedom to the nation's slaves.

While members of this latter assemblage may have supported the Union, many remained steadfast in their opinions that blacks were not ready—and perhaps never would be—for full citizenship, toward which freedom would certainly lead. Among this group were four Iowa families, the Earps, Curtises, Hamiltons, and Rousseaus, who had heard that California had a less liberal attitude toward political diversity than they witnessed where they were living in Iowa. As a result, throughout 1863 and into the early months of 1864, these four families prepared for a move out west.[1]

A decade before, Nicholas Porter Earp (1813–1907), patriarch of the legendary Earp clan that would include his sons Virgil, Wyatt, and Morgan, had already made his way to California and back. In later years he told the San Bernardino Society of California Pioneers (a group of former trappers, miners, and grizzly hunters who banded together for the purpose of preserving the history of San Bernardino County) that back in 1851 he had left his growing family in Iowa and joined the gold rush in northern California with the hope of bringing some of the "riches" back home.[2]

According to his testimony, after months of co-running a trading post near the mines at Hangtown (known today as Placerville), Earp was more than ready to return to Iowa. On the return trip he started out by taking an indirect route through southern California and crossing through the beautiful San Bernardino Valley, vowing that someday he would make it back to this wonderland of lush fertile fields, boundless timberlands, and deep, clear water streams.

Back in Iowa, Earp served as town marshal and later as assistant provost marshal. During 1863 and '64, the Earps and the other three families named above made plans and prepared to set out for California. Having made the journey before, Earp was selected captain of their wagon train.

The Earp family included Nicholas Porter, his wife, Virginia, their four sons James, Wyatt, Morgan, Warren, and their daughter Adelia. Another son, Virgil, was still serving in the Union army and would join them a short time later.

The Curtis clan made up the largest of the four family divisions in the wagon train. It consisted of the Reverend and Mrs. Israel C. Curtis; a married son, William Jesse Curtis, his wife, and their small son, Holman C. Curtis; and the unmarried children of the clergyman, including Richard, Emerine, Eliza A., Louis F., Alan V. Israel Jr., and Penelope. Also traveling with them were Stephen Thomas Hays and Mary Curtis Hays.

---

1. Nicholas Earp to James Copa, Letter, April 2, 1865, 4. The names of the families and individuals who made up the Earp wagon train (see p. 2) were recorded by Israel Curtis and his son William Jesse Curtis, both of whom traveled in the party. They, in turn, passed the names on to the Hon. Jesse W. Curtis Sr. (their grandson and son), who later confirmed them.

2. San Bernardino Society of California Pioneers, Record Book "A," January 21, 1888, through February 28, 1888.

Opposite, Rousseau diary. Courtesy of Mrs. Richard Molony.

"The Rousseau Diary and the Earp Wagon Train to San Bernardino 1864," *Overland Journal* (Fall 2015).

Evidence for the 1864 John Brown Family Camp Corral Sketch

Evidence and Items of Provenance from Larry Cundall

Personal contact information has been reduced or entirely redacted from this public document.

2/9/2024

Provenance Claim Re: Camp Sketch found in the 1864 Diary of Sarah Jane Rousseau, Area Found in Glendo, Wyoming

I, Larry Cundall, have reviewed the sketch found on the back pages of Sarah Jane Rousseau's 1864 diary **(See Attachment A)** and the accompanying written material provided for July 8-11 in *The 1864 Diary of Mrs. Sarah Jane Rousseau* and agree that both the sketch and written descriptions of her camps are compellingly similar to the landscape and geological formations found in the vicinity of Sawmill Canyon, Ragan Draw, and Sand Draw/South Fork Sand Draw in Glendo, Wyoming.

Specific evidence for the claim:

I. **I have reviewed the source material for both the Pella Company and Roe Train (including the Brown Train) and agree that their written descriptions and mileage estimates match the terrain and trail mileages for the following campsites:**

1. **July 8-9: Sawmill/Ragan Draw**
    a. The Roe Train and Brown Train most likely camped for the evening near the mouth of Sawmill Canyon or nearby at Ragan Draw, an accommodating area for a large gathering of emigrants with plenty of access to the North Platte River **(See Attachment B).**
    b. The Pella Company most likely camped for the evening on the North Platte River, near the mouth of Sawmill Canyon or nearby at Ragan Draw.

2. **July 9-10: Above Ragan Draw**
    a. The Brown Train most likely camped for the evening within a short distance (approximately 3-4 miles above the mouth of Sawmill Canyon). This matches a description offered in the Rousseau diary, saying the Browns/the New York Train had found "good grass and plenty of it." To do so, the emigrants likely had to travel beyond the more commonly frequented campsites, which would be picked over by stock animals in mid-July.
    b. The Pella Company camped for the evening in the same location as the Brown Train with a description in Sarah Rousseau's diary of having "sand for a carpet" and "high bluffs" surrounding them. This is a compelling description of the terrain found with 3-4 miles of Sawmill Canyon and Ragan Draw.

Evidence for the 1864 John Brown Family Camp Corral Sketch

3. **July 10-11: Alder Clump**
   a. The Brown Train is named in Martha Roe's diary as being present at Alder clump campsite where there are "high mountains" that can be comfortably hiked, and a nearby "spring." On July 11, Martha Roe expresses concern over having to travel "24 M[iles] without water," which I believe to be a near-accurate description of the trail conditions ahead from Alder Clump, with minimal exception.

   The Pella Company diarist claims to have traveled 8 miles from her prior camp, which reasonably brings her up through Sawmill Canyon into the vicinity of the Alder Clump camp. Sarah Rousseau claims to have passed, or more likely crossed "Alder Creek," which is one and the same as Boxelder Creek, which runs alongside the Alder Clump camp. She also claims there to be "over 20 miles of bad mountainous roads" ahead of her, which is a similar claim as seen in the Roe & Brown Train, suggesting they are in the same location, sharing the same concern.

   b. Additional Commentary: The description provided by Sarah Rousseau matches Andrew Child's 1852 description of the journey (less the detour to find grass), where he writes on page 22 of his guidebook, "7 ½ [miles] FINE BOTTOM between hills. [speaking of Sawmill Canyon] Some steep and bad descents before arriving at this place … one mile and a half further you come to ALDER CLUMP on the left of the road. Opposite to this is a spring of very cold water." **(See Attachment C).**

My personal credibility to make this claim

II. **I have personally visited the areas, reviewed maps at great length, or have seen other visual representations that match the terrain and contain evidence of trail use.**

   1. I am a local resident of Glendo, Wyoming and have occupied and worked a Angus Ranch that reached to the immediate vicinity of and included the Alder Clump campsite referenced in numerous trail diaries, such as the *1864 Diary of Mrs. Sarah Jane Rousseau*. **(See Attachment D).**

   2. My family has lived on and worked the same acreage my Great-Grandfather Harry Cundall homesteaded in 1917. The original settlement included the land between Broom Creek and Willow Creek. Presently under our control are areas including the Box Elder Spring, Buckcamp Spring, Spring Creek, and Spouting Springs, which all show visible signs of emigrant travel.

   3. I believe my family has responsibly stewarded the land since 1916 in a way that maintains the integrity of historically significant elements and I have personally contributed to the preservation and protection of occupant history such as gravesite recognition projects in collaboration with the Platte County Historical Society, Daughters of the American Revolution and the Oregon-California Trails Association. **(See Attachments F & H).**

   4. I have been fascinated by Oregon and Overland Trail history since I was a child and have researched the subject for over 60 years, as well as studying various archaeological findings on my own and neighboring lands.

a. Items of note that have been discovered on our land and stewarded by my family include:

- Folsom points dating back to 12000 B.C.E. and the remains of a mastodon that was excavated in the 1960s.
- The skeletal remains of Mrs. Ann Scott (at Alder Clump). **(See Attachment E).**
- The headstone and skeletal remains of a boy alleged name Jesse Cole (at Alder Clump). **(See Attachment E).**
- The skeletal remains of an Indigenous Woman and an infant presumed to be hers (at Alder Clump).

2. In addition to my own beliefs and observations, I have consulted with the following individuals who I consider to have sufficient expertise on the terrain and trail paths on their land and have informed me beyond my own personal experiences:

   a. Sandra Sommers, who grew up in and presently resides near Sawmill Canyon.
   b. Tim and Lisa Millikin, who presently reside in or occupy land near Ragan Draw and Sand Draw.
   c. Paul Henderson, a personal mentor and well-known authority on Western History and author of Landmarks on the Oregon Trail (1953). He served as a consultant for the National Geographic Society and was inducted into the Overland-California Trails Assoc.'s Emigrant Trails Hall of Fame in 2017. **(See Attachment G).**
   d. Dr. William Shay, former Western History instructor at Eastern Wyoming College and the first Assistant Historian under the leadership of Merrill Mattes at the Fort Laramie Historic site (1963-1970). **(See Attachment G).**
   e. Randy Brown, nationally recognized Oregon and Overland Trail historian, author of *Graves and Sites on the Oregon and California Trails* (1998) and *Inscriptions on Western Emigrant Trails* (2004), and trail preservation officer for the Wyoming chapter of the Oregon-California Trails Association.
   f. Susan Stafford, descendant of the 1852 trail diarist Abigail Scott Duniway and Ann Scott (who is buried on Alder Clump). **(See Attachment F).**

III. I have read numerous other trail diaries that contain mentions of the landscape and geological formations on the land I have either owned, occupied, or explored.

1. I have dedicated innumerable hours to researching and studying the people who have come through my property and have collected trail diaries, research articles, and other family accounts that have made me comfortable interpreting the material and placing the emigrants in specific locations on or near my property.

   a. Examples of diaries and entries that include similar descriptions of the land from Sawmill Canyon to Alder Clump:

   - 1852, Rev. John McAllister - "...arrive at Box Elders and an spring, good water, plenty dry cedar and pine... back opposite this to the right 1 miles is a natural fort bluff..." [at Alder Clump]

- 1854, Anna Maria Goodell - "We stopped where there are 4 or 5 springs…" [at Alder clump]
- 1852, Abigail Scott Duniway (who buried her mother Ann Scott at Alder Clump) - "The grave is situated on an eminence which overlooks a ravine intersected with groves of small pine and cedar trees; In about the centre of this ravine or basin, there wells forth from a kind of bank a spring of icy coldness, clear as crystal…"

2. My relatives have lived near me in the Sawmill Canyon area for many years and I have been privy to access on their land numerous times, both by on- and off-road means. I have explored the area with intent, following old wagon ruts and other trails on horseback.

3. I have personally retraced specific diarist's activities on foot and horseback, as well as driven to the sites described and visually confirmed the descriptions offered in such historical documents. Because of this, I am comfortable and feel confident identifying local camp sites that are mentioned in emigrant diaries and letters.

In Closing

Sarah Rousseau's diary sketch, accompanied by hers and complementary diary entries is a compelling depiction of the terrain and landscape found within a 4 miles radius from the head of Sawmill Canyon in Glendo, Platte Co., Wyoming. This claim is supported by map studies and in-person observations, in addition to my personal and learned knowledge of the area in question.

Signed,

Larry Cundall

Evidence for the 1864 John Brown Family Camp Corral Sketch

Related Attachments

Attachment A – Item of Reference

Depiction of a camp corral surrounded by bluffs found on pages Xa and Xb of the 1864 diary of Sarah Jane Rousseau. Molony Family Collection, Photographed by Nicholas Cataldo, 2015.

Evidence for the 1864 John Brown Family Camp Corral Sketch

Attachment B – Maps

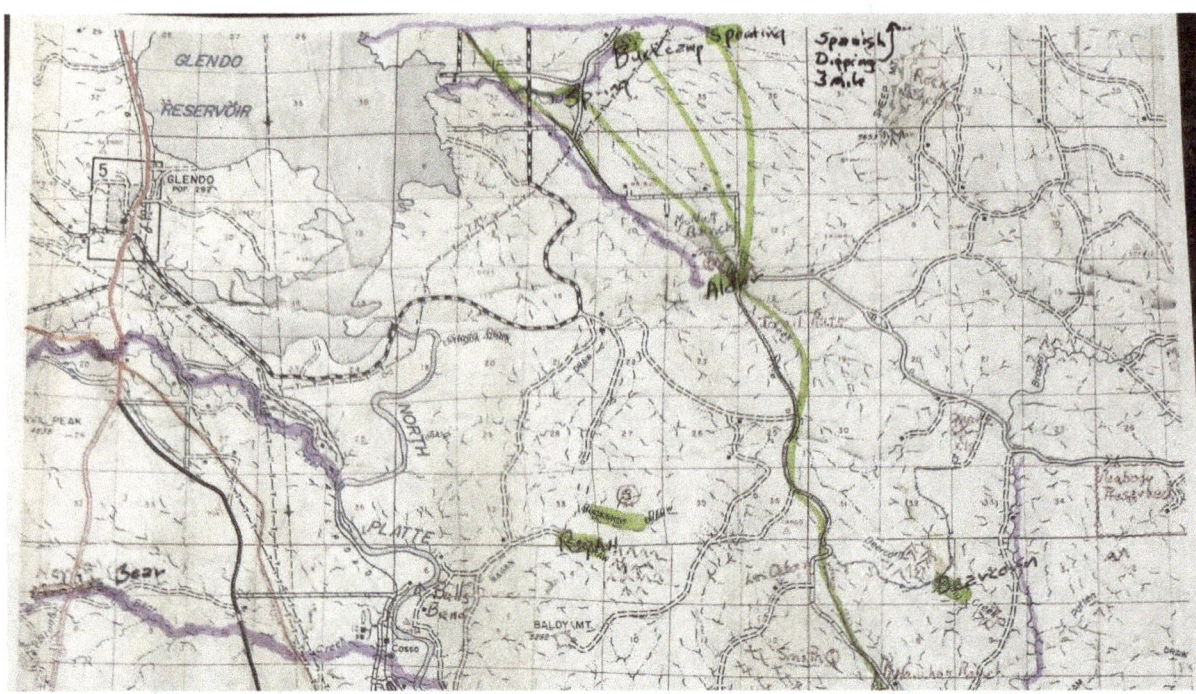

Map marked by Larry Cundall with trails and creeks labeled.

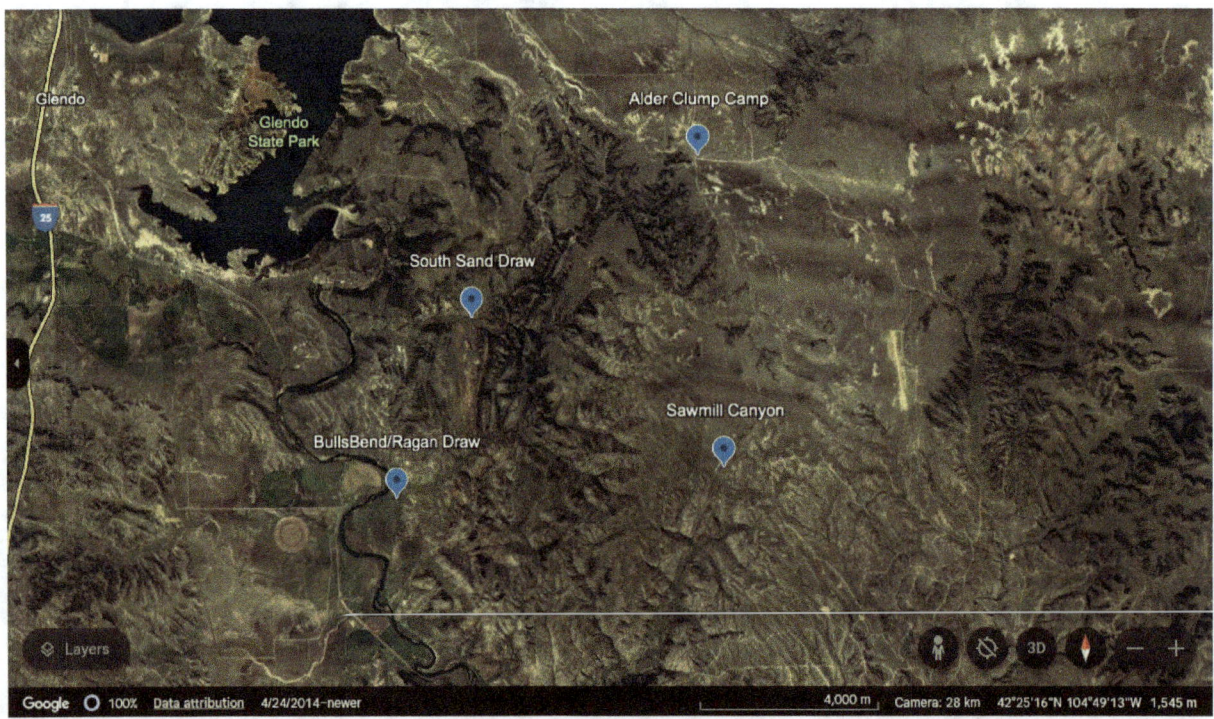

View of Glendo, Wyoming showing from views of Sawmill Canyon to Alder Clump.

Evidence for the 1864 John Brown Family Camp Corral Sketch

Attachment C - Relevant Pages from Andrew Child's 1852 Emigrant Guidebook

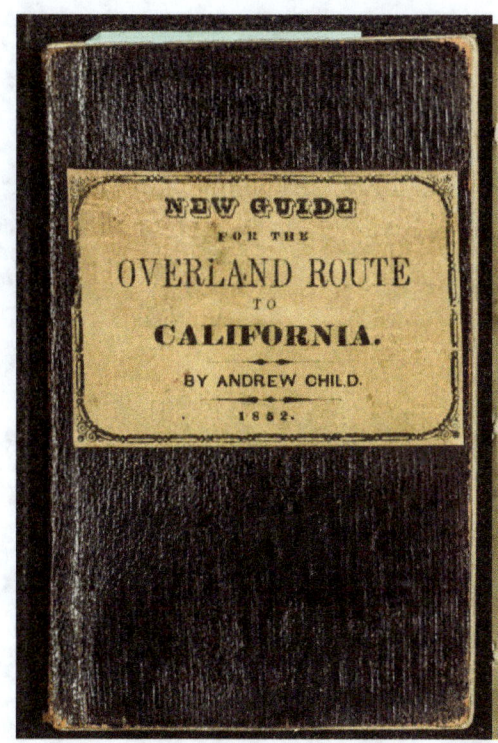

TO CALIFORNIA. 21

515¾ days in time upon those who here crossed to the south side, as nearly all of the emigration did. By this route we avoided twice crossing the Platte, and also the dreaded Black Hills of the south side. It must be added, however, that in very wet seasons, this route would be impracticable, on account of deep creeks, which we found dry. But in any *ordinary* season, as late as June 15th, I believe it to incomparably better than via the Black Hills of the south side. Four miles from the Fort is a

4 DRY CREEK and short steep ascent. The road the above distance runs near to river. It now leaves it for fourteen miles. Four miles and a half from "Dry Creek," is

4½ ENTRANCE TO PASS between mountains. The road to this point is, in many places, sidling and stony.

2½ GOOD COLD SPRINGS on the right of road, near to some young Cotton-wood trees.

7 ROAD JOINS RIVER. The last
533¾

22 OVERLAND ROUTE
533¾ seven miles is over a very rolling country. This point is a good place to camp, there being an abundance of cotton-wood timber, grass, and a spring which crosses the road. After leaving the last named point seven miles and a half, you come to

7½ FINE BOTTOM between hills.— Some steep and bad descents before arriving at this place, but we overcame them without difficulty, by careful driving. One mile and a half further you come to

1½ ALDER CLUMP on the left of road. Opposite to this is a spring of very cold water. Grass and wood is also here abundant. After a steep ascent from this place, the road is very sideling, over a flint and cobblestone hill, for one mile, to a

1 GOOD ROAD. This continues for three miles, gradually descending to a

3 CREEK, and one mile further is a

1 DEEP CREEK, which has a muddy bottom, but is not very bad to cross.—
547¾

TO CALIFORNIA. 23
547¾ For the next eight miles the road is tolerably good, but sandy in places, to the

8 RIVER. Here is good camping ground and plenty of timber and grass. The road is now rough, and after leaving river for four miles, it again

4 DESCENDS TO RIVER. The flat land near the river is sandy and barren, and the steep banks make it difficult to water teams. Four miles from here is a little feed near the river. Ten miles further is a

10 STEEP AND CRAGGY ASCENT Road mountainous. Five miles from here the

5 ROAD DESCENDS near to river. The road lies over a high rolling, and generally barren country, and is for the next fifteen miles, in sight of the river much of the distance, when you reach

15 LOW LAND bordering upon river. Here the grass improves, and in three miles more you reach the
589¾

Evidence for the 1864 John Brown Family Camp Corral Sketch

Attachment D – Alder Clump/Box Elder Creek Trail Marker

Still images from "Larry Cundall: A Real Wyoming Cowboy," filmed for Eastern Wyoming College's Communications Program, in partnership with Wyoming Humanities (Published on Dr. Bonelys Garage YouTube Channel, September 23, 2023).

Evidence for the 1864 John Brown Family Camp Corral Sketch

The trail marker was installed in 2017 by the Platte County Historical Society and the Daughters of the American Revolution.

Article excerpt from Sue Stafford, "Of a Certain Age…", for The Nugget, August 8, 2017.
https://www.nuggetnews.com/story/2017/08/08/news/of-a-certain-age/27536.html

Evidence for the 1864 John Brown Family Camp Corral Sketch

Attachment E - Emigrant Graves Discovered at Alder Clump/Boxelder Creek Camp

Article about the remains of the indigenous woman and infant found at Alder Clump in the Platte Co. Record-Times, 2001.

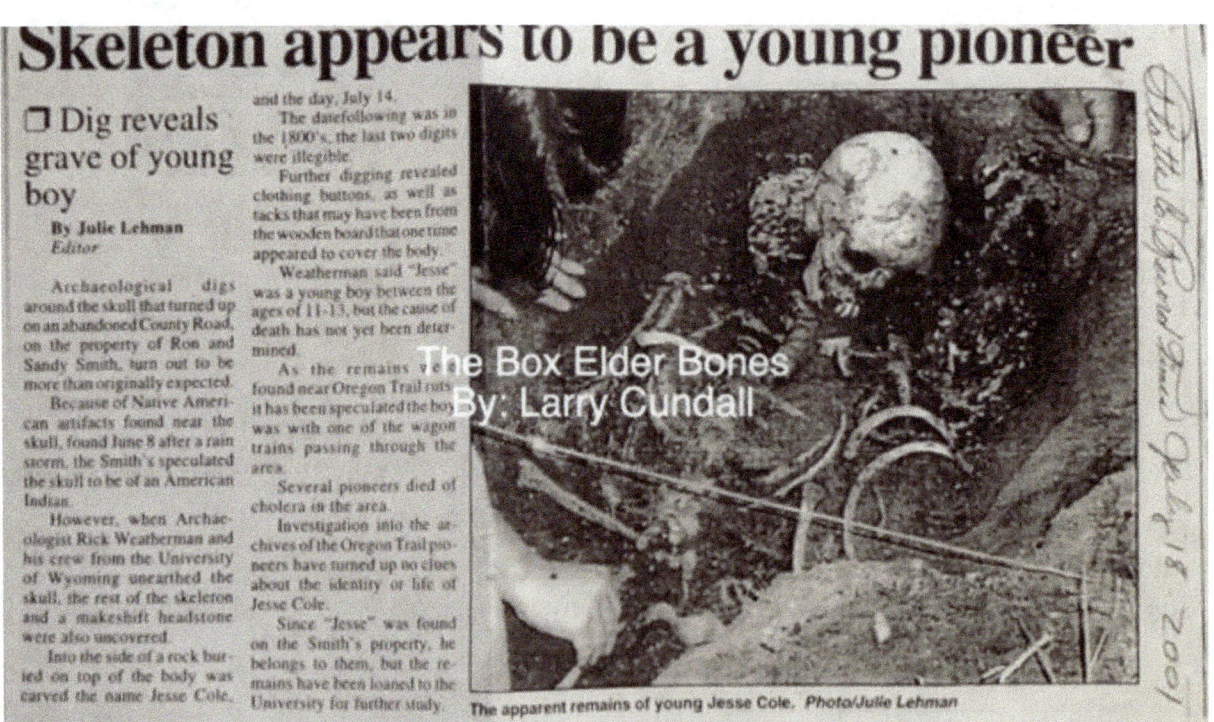

Article clipping from Platte Co. Record-Times of July 18, 2001.

8th Place- Jesse Cole Headstone, submitted by the Laramie Peak Museum, Wheatland.

It is the headstone of Jesse Cole who died July 3 or 4, 186? Three emigrate grave sites were discovered in 1970 and sent to the University of Wyoming to be studied. The Archaeologist identified them as two women and an adolescent boy – Jesse Cole. A sand stone rock with his name and death date were in his grave, with a board over all. The three skeletons were sent back to the landowner and the Platte County Historical Society. The decision was made to re bury them, wrapped in quilt tops, put into wooden boxes made by Wheatland Middle school students, May 2014 in a reverent ceremony. The committee decided to retain the head stone at the Laramie Peak Museum in Wheatland.

The grave site of may pioneers were suspected to be in the flat open meadow 20 miles east of Glendo, Wyoming known as Box Elder/Alder Clump where there is a flowing spring, good grass and wild roses blooming.

A skull was accidentally uncovered near the road headed to Hartville, WY. This is also known as Childs Cutoff of the Oregon/California/Mormon Trail. It is the trail many took to stay on the north side of the Platte River.

The committee from the DAR and the Historical Society had the decision to make – What do we do with these bones? The Archaeologist, Rick Weathermon preferred they be given back to his Department for studies/teaching. Everyone else was in favor of burying them. It was a different opinion for Jesse's head stone. The concern was of grave robbers. In the end the decision to put it in our museum in a glass covered wooden box where it would re respected and protected. It is a sorrowful reminder of lives cut short, journeys not completed.

A large metal sign is erected in the area explaining the use of this meadow, asking they respect the private-owned land and its important history.

Article excerpt about Jesse Cole in "Ten Best Wyoming Artifacts" by Buckrail.com, September 4, 2017. https://buckrail.com/10-best-wyoming-artifacts/

Evidence for the 1864 John Brown Family Camp Corral Sketch

Attachment F - Reinterment Ceremony in 2015

NEWS FROM THE PLAINS

Newsletter of the Oregon-California Trails Association

Summer, 2015   Volume XXX, No. 3

WYOMING CHAPTER

Around 150 lovers of Wyoming's historic trails turned out on a sunny Saturday in May for the reburial of the remains of three trails pioneers near a spring at Alder Clump on the Oregon/California/Mormon Trail, not far from the North Platte River.

The site - with a spring, trees and grass - has been used by people for millennia. Folsom points and mastodon bones dating back 12,000 years or more were discovered there in the 1960s.

In 1850, the heaviest year of travel on the trails, a group of emigrants chose not to cross the North Platte near Fort Laramie a few days after nine people had died at the spot trying to do so. Instead the travelers stayed on the north side of the river, pioneering a route that later came to be called Child's Cutoff.

The spring at Alder Clump, also called Box Elder, was attractive enough that nearly every party on the north-side trail either nooned or camped there. After a few years, enough people were buried at the site that some diarists called it a graveyard. Longtime Wyoming OCTAn Randy Brown and other researchers have discovered many trails diaries that describe the place or tell of events there. One of them may even recount the death of one of the people whose remains were reburied there in May.

Abigail Scott Duniway arrived at Alder Clump with her family on June 19, 1852. *"We are encamped this evening near some excellent springs which seen to gush from the rocks. We have good grass and wood and in a word have a very good camping place! ... The evening is pleasant and the sky is without a cloud."* But that night tragedy struck. *"How mysterious are the works of an all wise and overruling Providence! We little thought when last Sabbath's pleasant sun shed upon us his congenial rays that when the next should come it would find us mourning over the sickness and death of our beloved Mother!"* It was another case of cholera. Mrs. Scott took violently ill in the night and died the next afternoon.

Anne Roelofson Scott

In 1974, road construction near the site turned up the bones of a 25-33 year old woman. More bones eroded out of the ground at the site in 2001 and 2005. The skeletons have spent most of the years since their discoveries at the University of Wyoming's

Left to right, Project instigator Larry Cundall; his sister, landowner Robin Rankin; Randy Brown of Wyoming OCTA; and University of Wyoming anthropologist Dr. Rick Weathermon.

Anthropology Department, where they were closely studied by Dr. Rick Weathermon. The grave discovered in 2001 included remains of a 13- or 14-year-old boy, buried with a stone with the inscription "Jesse Cole July 14, 186?," the last digit in the year being illegible.

The remains discovered in 2005 were those of a woman aged 40 to 55, Weathermon noted during brief remarks at the ceremony. She could quite possibly have been diarist Abigail Scott Duniway's mother. The skeleton showed the woman had borne a number of children, and showed evidence as well that a recent birth had been particularly difficult, an infection had set in and the woman had continued traveling before she could properly heal, he said.

Afternoon activities included the Platte County Historical Society and the Daughters of the American Revolution, who unveiled a new historic marker at the site. Weathermon gave brief remarks; and landowner Larry Cundall spoke about the trails and ranching history of the area. The audience was treated as well to hymns, songs, a short homily and prayer from pastor and Wheatland Mayor Joe Fabian and remarks from Darla Teters of the DAR, Tamsen Hert of the Wyoming State Historical Society and Patsy Parkin of the Platte County HS. There also was a violin rendition of "Amazing Grace" by Erin Stoetz and a reading by MaryJo Birt from the Duniway diary. Sturdy, plywood boxes for the re-burial were built by Gendo Middle School 7th and 8th grade woodworking classes under the direction of their teacher Dean Finnerty.

Wyoming OCTA is especially grateful to Patsy Parkin and the Platte County Historical Society for organizing such a well-run, well-attended and fascinating event around the historic trails.   *--Tom Rea*

The remains were re-interred on my property in 2015.

2015 photo from Nancy Curtis with the caption "Randy Brown and Larry Cundall prepare to lower one of the boxes holding remains into the ground."

Evidence for the 1864 John Brown Family Camp Corral Sketch

Attachment G - Professors and Experts I've Learned From

Page from Eastern Wyoming College's 1969 yearbook with Dr. "Bill" Shay (left) and Paul Henderson (right).

In 1960 Mattes had urged the establishment of a second or assistant Historian position to take care of the burgeoning volume of business. Such a position was established on a 6-months appointment basis in 1963, being first filled by William J. Shay of Broomfield, Colorado, an old but energetic and highly motivated Army veteran, who remained seven years. Later he taught history at Eastern Wyoming College in Torrington, where he now resides. Jim Petty transferred back from another area to fill in as Curator behind Murray, and continues in that capacity to this day (1978). Sharp was able to brace his permanent staff with a second permanent clerk-typist, Beth L. Eaton. Lois Woodard was elevated to the role of Administrative Officer in 1960.

Relevant excerpt from Fort Laramie Park History by Merrill Mattes, 1980, section titled, "The Restoration of Fort Laramie."

Evidence for the 1864 John Brown Family Camp Corral Sketch

Fort Laramie—Old Bedlam

Emigrant Trails Hall of Fame
Oregon-California Trails Association

Paul Clifton & Mary Dunn Henderson

Biography

- Paul Clifton Henderson
  Born: 1895
  Died: 1979
- Mary Helen Dunn
  Born: 1898
  Died: 1988
- Married: 1923
- Railroad conductor (Paul); Homemaker (Helen)

Achievements

- Author, *Landmarks on the Oregon Trail*
- Impeccable lifetime study and mapping of the Oregon and Mormon Trails and other nationally significant trails.
- Instrumental in saving Fort Kearney, Fort Bridger, Fort Laramie and Fort Phil Kearny.
- Provided foundation for many others' trail research and documentation.
- Consultant for National Geographic Society and State of Wyoming

Paul and Helen Henderson are the Deans of Oregon Trail scholars, the spiritual forebears of OCTA, Oregon Trail scholars, and preservation advocates. The Hendersons worked as a team for more than 50 years to research, document, and map the Oregon Trail and other sites of western history. Most of their work was performed at personal expense, much of it during the Great Depression. Due to Paul's prodding, planning, and guidance, such notable trail sites as Ft. Phil Kearney, Ft. Fetterman, Ft. Bridger, Scotts Bluff National Monument, and Ft. Laramie were protected, restored, and expanded. Paul supervised the relocation of Joel Hembree's grave and facilitated the acquisition of South Pass City for the State of Wyoming.

Paul's *Landmarks on the Oregon Trail* stands alone as his only book, although he did contribute several articles to archaeological and historical periodicals such as *Nebraska History*. Yet, numerous trail scholars relied on the Hendersons' knowledge base, including government planners studying the feasibility of adding the Oregon Trail to the National Historic Trails System. Paul served more than eight years as a historic consultant for the Wyoming Parks Commission, despite being a Nebraska resident.

Their work continues to influence trail research today. Their records were donated to the Legacy of the Plains Museum in Gering, Nebraska, where researchers can study the hundreds of boxes containing nearly 375 diaries, letters, and journals, more than 10,000 slides and thousands of photos, clippings, correspondence, and numerous topographic, GLO, and personally drafted precise maps.

Paul Henderson's recognition in a 2017 issue of the *Overland Journal*.

Evidence for the 1864 John Brown Family Camp Corral Sketch

Attachment H – Honors and other recognition I've received for trail history preservation.

Evidence for the 1864 John Brown Family Camp Corral Sketch

Other Books in The Rousseau Series

The 1864 Diary of Sarah Jane Rousseau (2023). Sarah J. Rousseau's diary, supported with in-depth research notes, photographs, illustrations, maps, mileage and complete wagon train manifest and roster of all mentioned.

"An outstanding accomplishment!" – *BookFest* (2023 Winner)
"The most dramatic pioneer exploits of all." – *Tombstone Epitaph*
"Readers can go on an adventure through [Sarah's] eyes." – *The Oskaloosa Herald*
"A valuable account!" – *Arizona Journal of History*
"Of the hundreds of first-hand accounts by pioneers … [Sarah's] is among the most eloquent."
– *Overland Journal*
"Especially interesting to all teachers and students of the Westward Movement."
– *San Bernardino County Museum*

Emigrant Tales of the Platte River Raids (2023). Thrilling trail diary companion book featuring first-hand accounts and extensive research from the attacks of July 1864 in the "Black Hills of Idaho."

"A First-Rate Work of History!" - *WyoHistory.org* (Wyoming Historical Society)
"A treasure for anyone interested in this subject!" – *Arizona Authors Association*
An "important breakthrough in scholarship!" – *Western Association of Women Historians*
"Immersive" & "A Showcase!" – *IndieReader*
"Like stepping into a time machine…" - *Readers' Favorite*

From Where I Sat (Forthcoming). Fictionalized retelling of the Pella Company's 1864 Trip Across the Plains.

Evidence for the 1864 John Brown Family Camp Corral Sketch

www.ingramcontent.com/pod-product-compliance
Lightning Source LLC
LaVergne TN
LVHW061948070526
838199LV00060B/4031